THE CATHOLIC UNIVERSITY OF AMERICA
CANON LAW STUDIES
Number 93

THE SPECIAL MATRIMONIAL PROCESS IN CASES OF EVIDENT NULLITY

AN HISTORICAL CONSPECTUS AND COMMENTARY

A DISSERTATION

Submitted to the Faculty of Canon Law of the Catholic University of America in Partial Fulfillment of the Requirements for the Degree of

DOCTORATE OF CANON LAW

BY

EDWIN JOSEPH KENNEDY, J.C.L.,
Priest of the Archdiocese of San Francisco

THE CATHOLIC UNIVERSITY OF AMERICA
WASHINGTON, D. C.
1935

Nihil Obstat:

VALENTINUS T. SCHAAF, O.F.M., J.C.D.,
Censor Deputatus.

Washingtonii, D. C., die XVIII Maii, 1935.

Imprimatur:

✠ JOANNES J. MITTY, D.D.,
Archiepiscopus Sancti Francisci.

die XXIX Maii, 1935.

PRINTED BY
THE UNIVERSITY PRESS
BROOKLAND, D. C.

TO MY FATHER AND MOTHER

TABLE OF CONTENTS

PART II

COMMENTARY ON THE LEGISLATION OF THE CODE

CHAPTER III

CHAPTER IV

FOREWORD

This dissertation presents a study of the history of a certain process used to settle marriage questions—a process that was not always a trial, strictly so-called, and is known as the shortened or the summary process; in the second place is presented a commentary on this process as formulated in the Code of Canon Law. Marriage, a sacramental contract in the Church and an unique contract for the state, has always received special treatment. Because marriages are so sacred and so vital, one should conclude that they be treated with the greatest care, that the contract be not hastily made and that dissolution be granted only when the alleged causes have been established. To prove the reasons advanced for the dissolution, a full, formal trial might appear to be *always* required, lest the false be taken for the true; yet it must be admitted that some causes can be so easily demonstrated that the truth is practically self-evident. In such cases the reason for the lengthy procedure is absent, for then the establishment of the truth is not difficult; a formal process would be but a superficial burden on public authority and an unnecessary annoyance and delay for the parties who have a natural right to marry, a right that should not be denied nor suspended when the parties are evidently free and competent. Furthermore, marriage is to be considered not only as a sacred contract to be carefully safeguarded, but also as a state in which abuses may occur—serious abuses, for which both public and private interests demand a speedy remedy. These two reasons, the safeguarding of man's natural right and the remedying of abuses have ever obtained that a special, speedy or summary process be used for clear cases of null marriages.

Such a process has been studied in Roman and in Christian Law, with the emphasis placed on those tendencies toward a simplified process which received Papal approval in 1312 and again in 1889. Evidence will be proffered to establish that there has been a constant trend towards greater simplification, dating from the very occasion when Pope Benedict XIV prescribed a full trial with mandatory appeal in all marriage cases; before the Code, this trend had obtained the dispensation of the mandatory appeal and the simplification of the trial in the first instance; this trend has gone further with the Code which, it is believed, has sanctioned a very simple, administrative process for marriage cases of evident nulity.

The writer wishes to take this occasion to express his gratitude to their Excellencies, the Most Rev. Edward J. Hanna, D.D., and the Most Rev. John J. Mitty, D.D., for the opportunity afforded for advanced study. He also acknowledges with gratitude the helpful direction of the Faculty of the School of Canon Law and the assistance of Mr. James O'Neill in preparing the dissertation for the press; he also expresses his gratitude to all who have aided him in the preparation of this work.

PART I

HISTORICAL CONSPECTUS

CHAPTER I

THE SUMMARY FORM OF MARRIAGE TRIALS, DOWN to 1899

Article I. Roman Law

Under Roman law, the dissolution of marriages ordinarily was not handled by the courts. According to modern law, a sentence is required from a public official or magistrate or from the ecclesiastical judges, before a marriage is considered null or is dissolved. This differs completely with Roman law practice, which admitted that the spouses were competent to terminate their own mariage; this practice must be grasped to understand why the Roman courts ordinarily did not review marriage questions *de vinculo*. It is not necessary to dwell at length on the practice under ancient and ecclesiastical Roman law, because whatever influence came to eccleiastical procedure, was principally by way of the legislation of the Christian Emperor. In a few words, those marriages of the older Roman system in which the technicality of *manus* had been established by *confarriatio, co-exemptio* or *usus* were easily dissolved as long as this marital power was likewise broken; certain solemnities, *diffarreatio* and *remancipatio,* were the legal vehicles by which the effects of the initial contract were broken. There are texts which might indicate some sort of a court action, e. g., the *amicorum consilium;* at the most, these texts refer to a method of safeguarding the woman's interests and "there is a great gap between this and the conclusion that a rule of law existed calling for formal hearing and judgment in a court of the family."[1] It seems that another type of marriage existed in early Roman history—those which were "free" from the special feature of *manus*

---

[1] Dionysius, *Antiq.*, 2, 25; Plutarch, *Romulus,* 22; Valerius Maximus, 2, 9, 2; Corbett, *The Roman Law of Marriage,* 226-227.

("free", e. g., because of the *trinoctii absenta*);[2] for the dissolution of these unions, a mere statement of the parties or some symbolic action sufficed.[3] From the classical period on, marriages *cum manu* were no longer a matter of concern; the "free" marriages were the rule and were made by the mutual consent of man and woman who regarded each other with *affectio maritalis.*[4] To dissolve such marriages the parties could either agree that this *affectio* had ceased (divorce) or one could repudiate the other, using the *libellus repudii* (*repudium*), Although Emperor Augustus required by the *Lex Julia de Adulteriis* (18 A. D.) that the statement of the repudiation, written or oral, be witnessed by seven competent persons, this method of terminating marriages remained the affair of the parties themselves. Wanton repudiation and depravity resulted from this system and as a remedy the Emperors, especially from Constantine forward, enacted restrictions on the right of the parties to divorce or repudiate each other.[5] Justinian reordered many of the regulations of his predecessors, yet it remained the privilege of either party to repudiate the other for certain reasons or to agree to divorce;[6] thus, e. g., a wife could repudiate her impotent husband even though he did not wish a divorce[7] or a woman could enter a second marriage if it remained doubtful for five years whether her husband had been captured or had died.[8] It was only some years after the above regulations (in 542 A. D.) that Justinian abolished divorce by mutual consent (*bona gratia*) and even then admitted an exception if the parties did it "from a desire of chastity."[9] His son, Justin II, in 566 A. D. re-sanctioned divorce by mutual

[2] Gaius, I, 111.

[3] " . . . illam (mimam) suam suas res sibi habere iussit, ex duodecim tabulis clavis ademit, exegit . . ." Cicero, *Philip.*, II, 28.

[4] *Dig.* 23, 2, 5; *Code*, 5, 3, 6.

[5] *C. Th.* 3, 16, 1 and 2; *Code*, 9, 9, 34; *Code*, 5, 17, 8.

[6] *Nov.* 22, 4; CXVII, 12; CXXXIV, 11.

[7] *Nov.* XXII, 6.

[8] *Dig.* XXIV, 2, 6; Nov. XXII, 1.

[9] *Nov.* CXVII, 10; CXXXIV, 11.

consent, claiming that his father's decree was foreign to the times.[10] Accordingly with a brief interval of 20 years, marriages could have been dissolved by the mere agreement of a husband and wife to divorce; furthermore within the limits prescribed by the Emperors, i.e., by invoking one of the causes recognized in imperial edicts, any spouse could repudiate the other.

Ordinarily the intervention and sentence of a court were not required and the dissolution of marriages remained the affair of the parties themselves; yet, court trials involving the *vinculum* may well have occurred. For the protection of a wife's dowry, especially after a divorce or *repudium,* Roman law had the *actio rei uxoriae* which was practically fused by Justinian with the *actio ex stipulatu,* based on an implicit stipulation.[11] As this *actio* took final form under Justinian, a woman on the occasion of a divorce or *repudium* could claim restoration of her dowry, except where she had carried on improperly[12] or had repudiated her husband without one of the imperial causes;[13] in these latter cases, her property was forfeited to various uses. It is evident that at times there would have been a contest or discussion of these exceptions, requiring intervention and settlement by the courts; these would be called upon to decide, e. g., whether the woman really was an adulteress or whether her husband had forced her into this vice.[14] This is not a mere supposition but is confirmed by several references uncovered in the Novels. In one case, Justinian legislated that a year must pass before a woman may contract a second marriage: *"Sed etiam si mulier ex iusta causa repudium miserit et litem vicerit. . . illa quidem auferat lucra quae ante dicta sunt, erubescat autem prius quam annus transierit ad secundas nuptias migrare."*[15]

[10] *Nov.* CXL, 1.

[11] *Code,* 5, 13, 1; *Inst.,* 4, 6, 29.

[12] *Nov.* XCVIII, 1, 2.

[13] *Nov.* CXVII, 13.

[14] *Nov. CXVII,* 9.

[15] *Nov.* XXII, 16.

This rule was to hold, even though her first marriage had been dissolved because of some just cause; the text implies that she had brought her case to the courts and there had succeeded in establishing the validity of the cause for dissolution, (*litem vicerit*) an action which clearly was concerned with the *vinculum*. In another case, a new rule is specified to safeguard the validity of marriages contracted without the usual dowry or antenuptial gifts: the parties should testify before the *defensor ecclesiae* and several clerics that they had married and thereafter any offspring would be legitimate; and the wife, if she should serve a *libellus repudii,* could claim one-fourth of the husband's estate, if he ejects her from his home. The Emperor was brought to this legislation because such cases of injustice to the wife in non-dotal marriages were being carried to him constantly either as appeals of the first instance (Roman law) or as matters already heard in courts; again, of course, the implication is that courts had taken cognizance of a matter regarding the matrimonial *vinculum.*[16] Another instance is found in those cases where a husband or wife sent a *libellus repudii,* but did not invoke one of the approved causes of separation; here the judge was to consider the case and hand the guilty party, if a woman, over to the Bishop for incarceration in a nunnery.[17] Whether a *libellus repudii,* sent without one of the imperial causes, actually dissolved the marriage, is not certain; some have answered in the affirmative, believing the law to be merely penal, i. e., spec-

---

16 "Sed illud quoque ut apte ordinemus satius esse arbitramur, quod ex multa rerum experientia accepimus: certe *multae* et *continuae lites* ad nostram majestatem delatae ad praesentis nos legis necessitatem adduxerunt."—*Nov.* LXXIV, 4. "Quoniam ex aditionibus (interpellationibus) quibus semper petimur omnium quidem frequentissime mulieres conqueri et nuntiare audimus . . . '—*Nov.* LXXIV, 5.

17 " . . . si vero in eiusmodi impia voluntate perseveraverit et repudium marito miserit, iubems dotem quidem marito dari liberis communibus secundum leges servandam . . . ,mulierem vero *periculo iudicis* qui eam *causam cognoscat* episcopo urbis. . . . tradi, ut illius cura in monasterium immittatur usque ad finem vitae suae ibi permansura."—*Nov.* CXVII, 13; cf. *Nov.* CXVII, 15.

ifying punishments for transgressor,[18] but we believe that such an irregular *libellus repudii* did not dissolve the marriage according to Roman law and was penalized in addition. This second view appears sufficiently supported by the following Novel:

> Praedictas igitur omnes causas praesenti lege comprehensas solas sufficere iubemus ad solutionem legitimorum matrimoniorum, reliquas autem omnes cessare praecipimus, neque ullam aliam praeter eas quae nominatim huic legi insertae sunt posse legitimum matrimonium solvere, sive nostris sive antiquioribus continetur legibus.[19]

When such trials occurred, there is every reason to believe that they were governed by the ordinary rules of Roman procedure: they were not conducted in a summary fashion: this would seem to be supported since no special rules are found for this *actio ex stipulatu* nor for other matrimonial discussions.

ARTICLE II. EARLY CHRISTIAN PROCEDURE

As long as the *libellus* and mutual consent were admitted as approved methods of breaking marriages, there were bound to be abuses and depravity;[20] the wisdom of some obligatory court action in all marriage questions *de vinculo* is evident in view of those abuses and, since Roman law did not progress after this 6th century legislation, it would be well to stop and review the procedure that had been developing in the Christian communities, during these same centuries. How were marriage causes decided for these early Christians? In this discussion it is the *character* of the procedure that is to be considered primarily, rather than an outline of how the Church acquired rec-

---

[18] Buckland, *A Text-book of Roman Law*, 118.

[19] *Nov.* CXVII, 13; cf. *Nov* CXXXIV, 11.

[20] "Numquid iam ulla repudio erubescit post quam inlustres quaedam ac nobiles foeminae non consulum numero sed maritorum, annos suos computant, et exeunt matrimonii causa, nubunt repudii?—Seneca, *De Beneficiis*, III, 16.

ognition of her native jurisdiction in all matters connected with the Sacrament of Matrimony; yet this latter point must be introduced as it will throw light on the character of the procedure. Could it be said that the Roman law usage of private decisions was accepted by the Christians, whenever a question of a separation or of a dissolution of a mariage arose? Both the scriptures and the Fathers are witnesses against the adoption of this practice. No longer could the Roman Law *mutual consent* proceedings have sufficed after Christ clearly forbade the separation of validly married spouses for any cause except adultery and also forbade remarriage for all validly married, even when when the parties had been separated because of adultery.[21] Whether the use of the *libellus repudii,* without giving the right to remarry, was possible, can be discussed only for one case, adultery. It would seem from the context that this *libellus* (understood by the Jews and Romans, as permitting a second valid marriage) was also abolished, so that it would not ordinarily have been possible for the innocent party to depart at his or her own discretion. The same prohibition against the *libellus,* even though recognized by the State, can be found in the Fathers and in letters of the early Popes.[22] Since Christ abolished these two simple procedures for marriage causes, what course was to be followed by the early Christians when marriage questions arose? Evidently, some authority was to be invoked: it was to the Apostles and to the Bishops that the Faithful had recourse. The well-known cases decided by St. Paul for the Corinthians reveals this, viz., that case of the incestuous man and that of the status of a marriage contracted in infidelity when the pagan spouse refused to live peacefully with

---

[21] Matt. 19:9.

[22] St. John Chrysostom, *De libello repudii,* 1º—*MPG,* LI, 219. St. John Chrysostom, *In. Matt. Homil. XVII,—MPG,* LVII, 259. St. Augustine, *De Nuptiis et concupiscentiis,* I, 10,—*MPL,* XLIV, 420. St. Augustine, *Serm.* 392, c. 2,—*MPL,* XXXIX, 1710. Cf. reply of Pope Innocent I to the Bishop of Toulouse in 405; *Epis.* 6, *ad Exsuperium,* c. 6,—*MPL,* XX, 500.

the convert.[23] Furthermore, if the Christian spouses were to submit their marriage-plans for the approval of their Bishop, it is more than a mere conjecture that disputes, consequent to the marriage, were to be decided by the Bishops.[24] St. Paul had taken it for granted that the Christians should maintain their own tribunals[25]—an assumption that must have been quite natural to the convert, St. Paul, for he knew that the courts of the Jews were tolerated and even recognized as competent by the Romans.[26] Circumstances would hardly have encouraged those early Christians to submit their cases to the Roman courts because thus to seek a decision could easily have been fatal during the periods of persecution: because Roman jurisprudence did not regularly consider marriage as a matter for court action: because the laws of the Church for marriage were at variance with those of Rome.[27] After the persecution-period, the Bishops were recognized by Constantine as forming competent courts so that their decisions were binding and final;[28] although matrimonial questions are not explicitly mentioned, there is no reason to maintain that those were excluded from the Bishop's competence. This grant was confirmed by subsequent emperors, scil., by Arcadius and Honorius in 408 and by Honorius and Theo-

---

23 I Cor. 5: 7: 15-16.

24 "Decet vero ut sponsi et sponsae de sententia episcopi conjugium faciant . . ." Ignatius martyr, in Ep. *ad Polycarpum*, 5—*MPG*, V, 723: Cf. Albaspinaeus, "Reperi . . . in ecclesia olim statutum ne quisquam uxorem duceret, aut de nuptiis cogitaret, quin prius ecclesiam, id est episcopum . . . consuluisset eisque conditiones futuri conjugi, statum, religionem, sectam, patriam denique et aetatem exposuisset."—Perrone, *De Matrimonio Christiano*, II, 9, (3).

25 I Cor., 6:5.

26 Prat, *The Theology of St. Paul*, I, 104.

27 Cf. Pope Callistus permitting the marriage of Christian freed persons with slaves. Cf. St. Justin, *Apologia I, pro christianis*, c. 15—*MPG*, VI, 349. St. John Chrysostom, *Homil. XVI*,—*MPG*. XLIX, 164. St. Jerome, *Ep. LXXVII*, c. 3—*MPL*, XXII, 691. St. Augustine, *Serm.* 392, c, 2, —*MPL*, XXXIX, 1710.

28 *Cod. Theod.*, 1, 27, 1.

dosius II in 409.[29] In this same section of the Justinian Code, *de Episcopali audientia,* were included two special laws regarding marriage, thereby revealing that matrimonial causes were also viewed as within the Bishop's competence.[30] An actual case of this power in action (*facultati legum*) is that of Pope Innocent I having decided a second mariage as invalid, because of *ligamen,* in 410.[31] Before Constantine, then, Christians would have brought their marriage cases to Bishops for trial, probably secretly, without the sanction of the Roman rulers and after 313, the Bishops were official, fully recognized tribunals.

In the conduct of these trials, it would seem that the Bishops acted quite informally without the developed legal machinery of the contemporary Roman courts. Properly speaking, their action could not be called summary because there never had been a regular, formal trial in such cases, by comparison with which, the ecclesiastical procedure would have been summary. It is better to call that ancient Christian trial, informal or simple—similar, indeed, to what would be known later as the summary trial. It is not likely that the Apostles and Bishops would have borrowed Roman law's highly developed procedure in civil and criminal causes for their marriage trials; for, as has been seen, this procedure was not ordinarily used by the Romans for marriage trials and those difficult times were hardly favorable to the development and application of a full trial. Tests of the validity were not so frequent in those early days because impediments were fewer and the judgments, made by Bishops previous to marriages of the Faithful, surely prevented many invalid unions: hence, it could not have been from frequent practice that full juridical forms would have been developed. Those decisions rendered by St. Paul, at a distance, even dissolving a marriage, clearly were informally reached after the private review of the facts.

Authors, studying the development of the Church's exclusive

---

[29] *Cod. Theod.,* 1, 27, 2. *Code,* 1, 4, 8-9.

[30] *Code.* 1, 4, 16 and 28.

[31] *Epist. XXXVI,—MPL,* XX, 602-603.

jurisdiction in marriage questions, agree in admitting that this was not always and everywhere recognized in the following centuries. Marriages were tried in the courts of Christian rulers even by laymen: in these courts the rules were those of Roman, Germanic and Gallic law, i. e. of more or less developed juridical forms. It is to this mixing of jurisdictions that is to be traced the imposing of fuller juridical forms for marriage trials. Due to the contacts betwen the royal and ecclesiastical courts, the latter must have been affected by the more elaborate procedure of the secular tribunals. An evidence of this influence can be seen in Hincmar's account of a marriage trial at the Synod of Tousy (860): he censures the *actor*, Stephen, as juridically incapable of instituting an action because he had not appeared in person—a rule that reveals the introduction of juridical forms into ecclesiastical marriage trials.[32] Readings of the accounts of other Councils and synods before the 12th century, have failed to reveal traces or clues to other elements prescribed for marriage trials. These elements, in such evidence after the 12th century, must have been adopted *informally* in this or that tribunal, but never so universally that it could be said that the Church adopted the full Roman law procedure in her matrimonial courts. As shall be seen in the following chapter, even the revival of Roman law studies in the 12th century did not change this order for the whole church; marriage trials remained rather exceptional, prosecuted here with full legal machinery, and there informally. Although this revival of Roman law did not actually effect a *complete* change, it seems that the Popes of that time wished that the formal procedure of Roman law should have been the rule for marriage trials. Probably the best witness to this is Pope Innocent III who complained in 1188 that mar-

---

[32] "Unde licet talis accusatio non meretur synodaliter obtinere responsum quia nemo quemquam per scripturam absens potest *regulariter* accusare . . . "—Mansi, XV, 572.

riage cases were not being subjected to the regular procedure.[33] Two centuries later, in 1312, Pope Clement V sanctioned the use of a shortened or summary process for the whole Church, in certain cases including marriages. This was the first explicit and universal legislation for a summary process in marriage trials and reflected the practice and tendencies of the times that will be seen as characteristic of matrimonial trials in many places from the very beginning.

ARTICLE III. GRATIAN TO CLEMENT V (1044-1312)

In the first part of this article, are to be set down some of those forerunners, some of those tendencies toward summary treatment that occurred in the several centuries just preceding the 14th: in the second part, are to be reviewed the two decretals of Pope Clement V, *Saepe* and *Dispendiosam,* which were but the crystalization of the previous tendencies.

1. *Antecedents of the Summary-trial, in the 12th and 13th Centuries*

Due especially to the revival of Roman law studies in the 12th century, the full and rigorous requirements of Justinian procedure were demanded in many churches. Durandus (or Durantis), writing in 1276, remarked that criminal trials required the fullest hearing and that civil trials generally were also characterized by a full hearing.[34] Pope Innocent III approved a law passed by the IV Lateran Council (1215), requiring the presence of a notary at all trials, ordinary or extraordinary. The duties of this clerk, found in this same law, reveal what these formalities and "fullest hearings" were; it was these formalities

---

33 " . . . taliter respondemus, quod, licet ordo iudiciarius in aliis controversiis sit servandus, et in martimonialibus causis non usquequaque servetur . . . "—C. 1, X, *ut lite non contestata non procedatur ad testium receptionem vel ad sententiam deffinitivam,* II, 6.

34 " . . . quod regulariter in criminalibus plenissima causae cognitio requiritur." " . . . plena causa cognitio requiratur . . . generaliter in omnibus civilibus." Durandus, *Speculum Iuris,* Lib. I, Part I, *"De Officio . . . . Iudicum,"* §8, n. 2.

that he was to set down.[35] Marriage trials were not excepted from these same formalities, for they are not found in the lists which specify when the summary or speedy processes of Justinian Law could be used.[36] It was difficult however always to observe these requirements and they were the occasion of abuses or evasions of justice. Innocent III himself, answering a question about a trial at which the *reus* did not appear, though cited, remarked in 1198 that marriage cases were not being submitted to the regular procedure.[37] Parties who had appealed to Rome were often obliged to go there in person or send procurators and pay all those expenses consequent on the trip and residence and trial.[38] These cumbersome formalities gave lawyers and procurators opportunities to prolong the trial so as to obtain greater stipends.[39] Little wonder then, if Bishops proceeded without these rigorous formalities, especially in marriage cases, where the spiritual welfare of the parties was concerned: this

---

[35] " . . . qui fideliter universa iudicii acta conscribant, videlicet, citationes et dilationes, recusationes et exceptiones, petitiones et responsiones, interrogationes et confessiones, testium dispositiones, et instrumentorum productiones, interlocutiones et appellationes, renunciationes, conclusiones et cetera quae occurrerint, competenti . . . "—C. 11, X, *de probationibus,* II, 19.

[36] Durandus, *Speculum Iuris,* Lib. I, Part I, "De Officio . . . Iudicum", §8, n. 3.

[37] ". . . taliter respondemus, quod, licet ordo iudicarius in aliis controversiis servandus, et in matrimonialibus causis non usquequaque servetur . . . . "—C. 1, X, *ut lite non contestata non procedatur ad testium receptionem vel ad sententiam deffinitivam,* II, 6: Innoc. III Abbati sancti Proculi et L. Canonico.

[38] " . . . secundum locorum distantiam personarum et negotii qualitatem tempore prosecutionis indulto, si voluerit appellatus et petierit, principales personae per se vel procutores . . . accedant ad sedem apostolicam."—C. 1, *de appellat.,* II, 15, in VI°.

[39] "Illorum igitur onerosa multiplicitas et consequens difficultas propositum ordinem servandi, patulam adaperibant viam advocatis ac procuratoribus ad multiplicandas dilationes, exceptiones, cavillationes, iurgia et cetera omnia et quibus causae tractatio fieret longior et inde sibi notariis et sollicitatoribus, etc., uberiora emolumenta consequerentur.—Cerchiari, *Sacra Romana Rota,* I, 143.

was a fact admitted by Innocent III in 1209 when he was speaking of the necessity of a *litis contestatio.*[40]

Besides these general references to a shortened procedure, there are traces of particular exceptions dating from the very period of the renewed interest in Roman law. These instances are not always general papal dispensations, but even in private cases, they indicate the desire of the Popes to render judgments in marriages cases more expeditious. It is worthy of note that in his study of the early history of the Roman Rota, Cerchiari arrives at a similar conclusion for that body, remarking that the Roman Pontiffs often used the words *simpliciter, et de plano, sine strepitu iudicii et figura*—the phrase which was to be the backbone of Clement V's legislation.[41]

For the sake of clearness, the order of a trial and not the chronological order, will be followed in reviewing these exceptions to the strict Justinian procedure. It is interesting to learn that the important *Libellus conventionis* was not always demanded in marriage cases. A written *Libellus* was the rule, but authors of the 13th century in recommending it had to acknowledge a contrary custom. When a woman petitioned against her husband or vice versa, or if a marriage was to be denounced, Hostiensis remarked that some courts did not demand a written

---

[40] "Tunc etenim, ne . . . viro sive mulieri fornicationis occasio praebeatur, maxime quum propinquitatis gradus opponitur lege divina prohibitus, in huiusmodi casibus, si videlicet contumax apparuerit is in quem fuit actio dirigenda . . . testes, lite non contestata, sunt merito admittendi et . . . ad deffinitivam sententiam procedendum."—C. 5, X., *ut lite non contestata non procedatur ad testium receptionem vel ad sententiam deffinitivam,* II, 6.

[41] "Huc quidem spectarunt varie iudiciorum formae a Papa in specialibus commissionibus statutae, quarum vestigia facile reperiuntur in relative paucis Capellanorum nostrorum actibus qui romanorum Pontificum Regestris inserti reperiuntur. Ast, denique persuasum habuerunt Papae utile quidem esse iudices et litigantes ab observantia iuris solemnitatum solvere, causas frequenter committendo cum clausula: *simpliciter et de plano, sine strepitu iudicii et figura,* quam ante finem saeculi XIII non semel in commissionibus appositam reperimus."—Cerchiari, *Sacra Romana Rota,* I, 140.

statement.[42] For all matrimonial causes, Durandus, too, demanded a written statement of the case, but he had to admit a contrary practice:[43] it is pertinent to add that Joannes Andrae in the accompanying *Glossa* remarked that this contrary custom had been incorporated in Clement V's constitution.[44] From another point of view the *Libellus* was omitted, i. e., when the Bishops proceeded against marriages *ex officio*. At times well founded rumors served as the accuser of illicit unions in absence of any personal denunciation: in such cases, a Bishop could set a trial in motion, even without having received the customary written accusation. Pope Alexander III admitted this form of action as early as 1170 in his answer to the Bishop of Amiens, regarding a marriage invalid because of consanquinity.[45] Writing in the following century, both Hostiensis and Durandus present this mode of proceeding as accepted and regular; both authors warn Bishops to proceed carefully lest an injustice be done, especially when no one appears to defend the marriage.[46]

---

42 "Si mulier petit aliquem in virum et a contra: licet secundum consuetudinem quarundem ecclesiarum non porrigatur, libellus, tamen melius est et tutius quod detur, ita quod is qui impeditur scit a quo et super quo et qualiter et sic deliberet. Quia libellus est de substantia iudicii."—Hostiensis, *Summa,* Lib. IV, "Qui matrim. accusare possunt," n. 1. "In summa notandum est quod denunciatiuo aliquando fit in scriptis, aliquando sine scriptis sed melius et tutius est ut in scriptis fiat sicut dici supra." Hostiensis, *Summa,* Lib. IV, "Qui testes requirantur," n. 3.—Durandus, *Speculum Iuris,* Part IV, "Qui matrim. accus.", §2, n. 6; §2, n. 9.

43 "Postremo illud notandum est quod causa matrimonialis per discretum et literarum iudicem est tractanda . . . et libellus in ea dandus . . . nec laudo in hoc contrariam consuetudinem."—Durandus, *Speculum Iuris,* Part IV, "De Spon. et Matrim.", §6, n. 1.

44 "Hodie per Clem. *de verb. signifi saepe,* non est necesse libellum offerri: detur tamen petitio in actis scribi . . . " Joannes Andrae Glossa ad *Consuetudinem,* in Durandi, *Speculum Iuris,* §6, n. 1.

45 ' . . . respondemus quod . . . tui officii interest matrimonia illa adhibita gravitate dissolvere quae illicita contracta noscuntur."—C. 3, X, *de divortiis,* IV, 19.

46 "Verum Episcopus ex officio inquirere potest, si infamia orta est . . . et facit quando aliquis accusat nullus appareat defensor: . . . Iudex autem quando ex officio procedit actore apparente et nullo defensore com-

Ordinarily, however, a *Libellus* was required, as pertaining to the very substance of a trial; in the composition of this document, a formality that is thought to have come from Justinian procedure was mitigated. Under early Roman law, formalism was so essential that its neglect rendered a trial null;[47] even in Justinian's time, the lawyer had to cast his client's case into some one of the accepted *actiones,* according to the view of the majority of Romanists,[48] a view that seems to receive confirmation from the following action of a Pope in the 12th century. In 1160, Alexander III spoke strongly against the subtle, delaying practice of searching out some *actio* in which to present the case. "Sedulously should" his questioner, an English Bishop "look simply for the fact itself and establish the truth, avoiding legal subtleties." In the *Glossa,* this particular response is cast into a general principle: ". . . It suffices for the actor to propose the fact nor is he obliged to express the name of the *actio.*"[49]

Another departure in this period followed upon the the regular presentation of a *Libellus* and citation of the parties, viz., the trial sometimes proceeded without a *litis contestatio,* even to a final sentence. Ordinarily, the cause of this exceptional action

parente debet esse cautus . . . "—Hostiensis, *op. cit.,* IV, "Quae except. competant . . . " n. 3. " . . . idipsum (scil. 'de plano, ex officio suo inquirat'), etiam potest facere nullo accusatore apparente, infamia super hoc orta, ut dixi, citatis tamen quos tangit et publicata accusatione . . . "—Durandus, *Speculum Iuris,* Lib. IV, Part IV, "Qui matrim. accusa., §2, n. 5.

[47] Gaius, 4, 11.

[48] "Un seul point reste a verifier et qui est sujet a controverse. La voie de droit exercee par le demandeur (soit), l'action indiquee par son nom technique . . . avait ete communiquee . . . durant *l'editio actionis* extrajudiciaire. La *postulatio* simplex reproduisait-elle le moyen designe? Il semble que non."—Collinet, *La Procedure par Libelle,* p. 288.

[49] "Provideatis attentius, ne ita subtiliter sicut a multis fieri solet, cuius modi actio intentetur, inquiratis, sed simpliciter et pure factum ipsum et rei veritatem secundum formam canonum et sanctorum Patrum instituta investigare curetis." Glossa ad *Dilecti filii*—"Sufficit actori factum proponere nec cogitur nomen actionis exprimere."—C. 6, X, *de iudiciis,* II, 1.

was the contumacy of the defendant; if for any of a number of reasons the cited party refused to appear, the discussion and decision of the disputed marriage was to be undertaken. In a reply of Innocent III (1188), it is indirectly seen that this exception was taken for granted. A woman had sought a separation from her husband because of his adultery; despite the latter's refusal to appear and answer, the court had heard witnesses and was puzzled whether it should pass the sentence. The Pope replied that, "*since it is not a question of the marriage bond*, but only of a separation, the judge could not proceed to the sentence because of the lack of the *litis contestatio*."[50] In his very denial that a judge should permit a separation from a contumacious and adulterous spouse, the Pope implicitly admitted that in other matrimonial questions, a trial could be valid, even without *litis contestatio*. That the *litis contestatio* was not always necessary in questions concerning the marriage bond,, becomes clearer from another general reply of Innocent III in 1209. Having firmly insisted on the necessity of the *litis contestatio* ordinarily, this Pontiff admitted exceptions, e. g., when one of the parties had been proved contumacious.[51] In their writings of a few years later, both Hostiensis and Durandus admitted as a general rule that a judge could proceed to a definitive sentence, even though no *lis* had been established, due to the contumacy of one of the parties.[52] It is interesting to note that

---

50 " . . . respondemus . . . quia tamen in praesenti negotio non est actum *de foedere matrimonii*, sed de crimine adulterii, per quod ad separationem coniugii non ad coniunctionem intenditur, quia lite non contestata testes fuerint recepti, et attestationes etiam publicatae, sive deferendum sive non deferendum appellationi fuisset, non est ad diffinitivam sententiam procedendum."—C. 1, X, *ut lite non contestata non procedatur ad testium receptionem vel ad sententiam deffinitivam*, II, 6.

51 C. 5, X, *ut lite non contestata non procedatur ad testium receptionem vel ad sententiam deffinitivam*, II, 6.

52 "Item ubi agitur de matrimonio . . . carnali et is, cuius matrimonio agitur, abeat, si *contumax* fit vere vel presumptive recipiuntur testes, et fertur deffinitiva sententia."—Hostiensis, *Summa*, II, "Ut lite non contest.," n. 2. "Certum libello oblato, coniuges citabuntur: dabuntur iudiciae legitimae ut . . . fiet litis contestatio: iurabitur de veritate dicenda . . . alias

in his *Glossa* upon this passage of Durandus, Joannes Andreae remarked that in his day the two Clementine constitutions (of 1312) were the rule for such cases.[53]

Since Benedict XIV's constitution *Dei Miseratione*, a *defensor vinculi* has been necessary for marriage trials: but even before this Pope, efforts had been made to safeguard the sanctity of the sacramental bond, without the insistence on a special office. Experts, frequently the *canonici*, were to assist the Bishops in their judgments:[54] and even persons, interested in a marriage case, could defend it in court. Yet these safeguards were dispensed with at times, so that a judge could proceed to a sentence without having heard any one pleading for the marriage bond. Thus Alexander III in the 12th century had established it as a general rule that a Bishop could dissolve a union, recently contracted, but invalid because of consanquinity, without having heard his adviser or *canonicus*.[55] Another rule was as follows: if the parties did not wish to appear in court, the accusation was to be published so that some friend or even some stranger might defend the bond; yet again a simplified action was permissible, scil., if no one appeared, the judge would evaluate the evidence and pass sentence, informally.[56]

---

sententia non valebit . . . nisi forte contumaciter abisset." "Quod si fiat accusatio super foedere matrimonii . . . tunc procedetur lite non contstata: secus, si propter adulterium ad thori separationem agatur."—Durandus, *Speculum Iuris*, Lib. IV, Part IV, "Qui matrim. accus.," §2, n. 5.

[53] Glossa in Durandus, *Speculum Iuris*, Lib. IV, Part IV, "Qui matrim. accus.," §2, n. 5.

[54] Recall the frequent inscriptions on responses from Rome. "Exonensi Episcopo et Capitulo Londonensi: C. 6, X, *de iudiciis* II, 1; Abbati Sancti Proculi et L. Canonico: c. 1, X, *ut lite non contestata non procedatur ad testium receptionem vel ad sententatiam deffinitivam*, II, 6.

[55] Si vero matrimonium ipsum est recenter contractum . . . fama viciniae et personorum sollicite perscrutata, causam audias et eam sine canonico studeas terminare."—Compil. I, Lib. IV, Tit. XI, *qui matrim. accusare possunt vel testificare*. C. 18, X, *de recriptis*, I, 3: Innocent II, "sine canonico."

[56] "Si vero hi nolunt venire vel defendere, dixit dominus meus quod accusatio est in ecclesia publicanda ut si quis cognatus vel amicus vel . . .

After sentence had been passed—at times in an informal manner, without the customary solemnities—[57] the party, who so desired, could make an appeal, though this was not necessary, as Benedict XIV later required. To bring some marriage cases to a speedier termination, this right of appeal was denied, as is evidenced by the phrase *remota appellatione* in particular Papal responses found throughout *C. I. Canonici* and in the later compilations.[58] Pope Gregory IX in 1234 gave several answers that seem to embody general principles prohibiting appeals in cases where the crime or impediment was quite evident. Thus, the first decision was to be final when it was manifest and notorious that a man was living with a woman who was another's wife;[59] or when the crime of *raptus* was most evident;[60] or when an appeal had been placed so that the party could continue in his notoriously sinful relation.[61] In this might be seen a foreshad-

---

quilibet extraneus velit defendere matrimonium admittatur . . .quod si nullus defensor appareat . . . iudex divortii sententiam proferat inter coniuges."—Durandus, *Speculum Iuris,* Lib. IV, Part IV, "Qui matrim. accus.," §2, n. 5.

57 " . . . iudex ratione praevia de plano ex officio inquirat et probato coram eo legitimo impedimento debita gravitate adhibita sentatiam divortii profert inter coniuges."—Durandus, *Speculum Iuris,* Lib. IV, Part IV, "Qui matrim. accus.," §2, n. 5. C. 3, X, *de divortiis,* IV, 19: Alexander III.

58 Compil. II, Lib. IV, Tit. XII, c. 1; cf. following footnotes.

59 "Aliquando aliqui quos manifestum sit et notorium uxorem alterius detinere . . . appellaverint, eorum appellationi non est aliquatenus deferendum . . ."—C. 14, X, *de appellationibus, recusationibus et relationibus,* II, 28.

60 "Praeterea si raptor sit . . . qui appellat, huiusmodi appellatio facta in iudicio apud ecclesiasticas personas solet audiri, *nisi* forte manifestus (manifestissimus) raptor vel fornicator existat."—C. 5, X, *de appellationibus, recusationibus et relationibus,* II, 28.

61 Si vero eorum excessus publicus est et notorius, appellationis obtentu, si quemadmodum iniquitatem fovendam interposuerit, non praetermittas quin eos excommunicatos denuncies . . . donec passis iniuriam satisfaciunt . . ."—C. 13, X, *de appellationibus, recusationibus et relationibus,* II, 28.

owing of our present exemption from an obligatory second trial and sentence.

2. *The Decretals, Saepe and Dispendiosam, of Clement V*

The outlining of these exceptions, that found place in the court practice of the 12th and 13th centuries, leads naturally to the decretals published in 1312, by Pope Clement V.[62] Wishing to reduce the lengthy and involved proceedings for a number of cases, including marriages, Clement V published his decretal, *Dispendiosam,* in 1312.[63]

With these few words, *procedi valeat de cetero simpliciter et de plano ac sine strepitu iudicii et figura,* a brief and final trial was sanctioned for marriage cases. This law, known by its first word *Dispendiosam,* was of wider application than later summary processes: for it embraced all matrimonial causes, practice deciding in favor of the inclusion of *separatio a mensa et toro propter adulterium,* although the Glossator had remarked that it was not certain that such a question was to be settled in this summary fashion.[64]Again, it was not only *evident* cases that resort could be taken to this shortened trial; for the constitution made no distinction based on the clearness of the cause; all marriage questions could be thus settled, as long as the truth was finally established. This summary character could mark all subsequent proceedings; if with good reason, an appeal were

62 "Quapropter sapientissime Clement V in scriptam firmamque legem quod *ius consuetudine* forte obtinuerit, redigens, *Dispendiosam . . .*" Cerchiari, *op. cit.,* I, 143.

63 "Dispendiosam prorogationem litium . . . restringere in subscriptis casibus cupientes, statuimus, ut in causis supra electionibus . . .quibusvis beneficiis ecclesiasticis necnon supra matrimoniis vel usuris, et eas quoque modo tangentibus, ventilandis, procedi valeat de caetero, simpliciter, et de plano, ac sine strepitu iudicii et figura."—C. 2, *de iudiciis,* II, 1, in Clem.

64 Cf. *supra,* p. —where Pope Innocent III held for a strict procedure in adultery cases. Glossa ad *Matrimonium:* "Videtur quod constitutio locum non habeat." "By the law of the Church, as enacted by Pope Clement V (1312), the trial or judicial proceedings in all matrimonial causes whatever, whether they relate to divorces from bed and board . . . can be summary."—Smith, *Ecclesiastical Law*; Vol. II, n. 1423.

taken—an action permitted under the *Dispendiosam*—this second instance could also be summary in its proceedings.[65]

From the beginning of this new procedure, there was no doubt whether this summary trial was obligatory or not; it was clearly, not obligatory.[66] At times, one party wished the full, formal trial, which was not desired by the second party; in such cases, the judge was to clear the way by an interlocutory sentence with the presumption to favor the summary process, because it had been established as a special remedy by law.[67]

Although there may have been little doubt as to the occasion on which this brief process was permissible, there were doubts concerning the composition or procedure of summary trials. To answer these questions Pope Clement V published another constitution, *Saepe,* in which he explained the meaning of *simpliciter, de plano* . . . etc., outlining just which acts should be eliminated and which retained.[68] Briefly, the Pope required the observance of those fundamental acts that would safeguard the justice of every case; viz., 1) citation, 2) oaths against falsehood and giving guarantee of speaking the truth, 3) proofs pro and con, 4) questioning of the parties by the judge, and 5) rendering of the sentence, after the parties had been cited. So that these trials should more surely be speedy, the following restrictions were enjoined: 1) a simple verbal statement of the point at issue, was to replace the elaborate, formal *Libellus conventionis,* 2) no *litis contestatio* was required, 3) the number of exempt days was reduced so that sessions could be held more

65 "Sextus est effectus quod per dictam clausulam causa efficitur summaria non solum in prima instantia, verum etiam in aliis instantiis usque ad finem litis."—Pellegrini, *Praxis Vicariorum,* 114, n. 5.

66 Glossa ad *Valeat:* " . . . non dicit *debeat:* per quod patet judex potest etiam contradicentibus partibus servare iudiciarium ordinem in causis praedictis." "Partes posse petere a iudice ut procedatur iudicio ordinario." Lega, *De Iudiciis Eccles.* I, 1, n. 598.

67 " . . . a iudice per sententiam interlocutoriam praeiudicialem hoc determinandum est." *ibid.,* n. 598. Glossa—*Casus:* " . . . iudex potest procedere summarie—vel etiam si potest observare ordinem iudicarium."

68 C. 2, *de verb. signif.,* V, 11, in Clem.

frequently, 4) useless *exceptiones* were not to be countenanced, 5) the *conclusio in causa* was not essential, 6) the sentence, though written, should be delivered howsoever it pleased the judge, 7) appeals to delay the conclusiveness of the sentence, were not to be admitted.[69] From a reading of this resumé of the decretal, *Saepe,* it would seem that the summary trials were to be brisk and informal, unhampered by cumbersome, legal machinery, and this, even in the first instance. It hardly seems that Pope Clement V intended to make the summary process merely administrative; sufficient characteristics remained to warrant the calling of the new method an abbreviated judicial process.[70]

ARTICLE IV. BENEDICT XIV'S CONSTITUTION *Dei Miseratione.*

1. *Relation to Clement V's Decretal Saepe.*

From this period (1312) till Benedict's legislation, there do not appear to have been any legislative changes in the summary processes used in matrimonial causes. Various authors writing during these centuries, continued to number marriages among the causes exempted, by law, from the formalities of an ordinary trial.[71] Not everywhere was this concession used or at least it was not used fully, in such wise that some of the optional solemnities were still observed when a summary process was being professedly followed; hence the traces of a proceeding known as *mixti ordinis.*[72] Whilst the summary process was not changed by

---

69 *De Iudiciis Eccles.,* Lega, I, 1, n. 597. Smith, *Eccles. Law,* II, n. 1269-1271. *Praelectiones I. C. Sancti Sulpicii,* III, n. 685.

70 "Nothing, however, can be omitted in summary trials that is essential to judicial proceedings." Smith, *Eccles. Law,* II, n. 1270; n. 1265. " . . . iudicium summarium procedat a jurisdictione contentiosa nec a iudiciis ordinariis differat nisi ratione . . . solemnitatis."—*Praelectiones . . . Sancti Sulpicii,* III, n. 684.

71 Pellegrini, *op. cit.,* 114, n. 8; Reiffenstuel, *Jus Canonicum,* Lib. II, Tit. I, *De Iudiciis,* §II, n. 47.

72 " . . .post latas clementinas constitutiones praxis iudiciorum tribunalis Rotae, dum mordicus adhaesit clementinis praeceptis, non omnes tamen abiecit veteres solemnitates, ita ut vere vocari possit et debeat mixtus iudicialis ordo . . . " Cerchiari, *Sacra Romana Rota,* I, 145, n. 44.

law, it suffered abuses in the way of hasty, unwarranted decisions—a thing that Clement V must have foreseen when he wrote: *Non sic tamen iudex litem abbreviet, quin probationes necessariae et defensiones legitimae admittantur.*[73] For the existence of this unfortunate abuse, the best evidence is found in the introductory sentences of Benedict XIV's constitution *Dei Miseratione,* a witness of the 400 years of matrimonial procedure since the introduction of Clement's summary process. Pope Benedict complained:

> Ad aures Apostolatus Nostri pervenit, in quibusdam ecclesiasticis Curiis inconsulta nimis iudicum facilitate infringi, et temere atque inconsiderate de eorumdem matrimonium nullitate litis sententiis, potestate conjugibus fieri transeundi ad alia vota: . . . qui . . . proclives sunt ad matrimonia dissolvenda, atque eadem matrimonia levi vel etiam nullo habito examine, irrita ac invalida declarant.[74]

It was to remedy such abuses that this Pope set up new requirements in matrimonial procedure. Here a detailed analysis is not to be made of the constitution *Dei Miseratione,* but rather a comparison of Clement's decretal with Benedict's constitution to determine whether the latter destroyed the concessions of the former or whether a summary marriage trial was still permissible after November 3, 1741. There is no explicit reference in the constitution *Dei Miseratione* to Pope Clement's decretal nor does the matter treated offset, point by point, the entire content of the decretal *Dispendiosam.* The latter empowered the judge to deny useless appeals—*appellationes dilatorias et frustatorias* [75]—when, e. g., the nullity was notorious or evidently established. It is this feature alone that Benedict XIV clearly changed, when he required that an appeal always and necessarily be taken from a first sentence favoring nullity and

---

[73] C. 2, *de verb. signif.,* V, 11 in Clem.

[74] §1 and 3—Fontes, n. 318.

[75] C. 2, *de verb.* signif., V, 11, in Clem.

this, regardless of the conclusiveness of the evidence.[76] As a consequence the parties were free to enter a second marriage, only after two sentences favoring the nullity of their first union—whereas Clement V would have this permission granted after a single trial.[77] Another solemnity was introduced by Pope Benedict XIV, viz., the necessity of a special officer, the *Defensor Matrimoniorum*: he had to be present at every marriage trial when the validity of a bond was in question,[78]thus replacing the arbitrary presence of a person or persons interested in defending the marriages, as from the 12th century on (*Supra,* p. 18), this point of legislation is over and above Clement's rather than a change from it.

Apart from these two characteristics, there can not be found any, even indirect, references to Pope Clement's decretal, so that it would seem rather clear that the summary trial could have still been used. In fact, many authors writing before 1889, have maintained that, "even matrimonial causes of nullity may at present be tried summarily, so far as this summary procedure is compatible with the observance of the peculiar formalities laid down in said constitution, *Dei Miseratione.*"[79] Opposing this rather common opinion, there was a more cautious view that urged observance of the full solemnities of an ordinary trial, this

---

[76] " . . . sin autem contra matrimonii validitatem sententia feratur, defensor inter legitima tempora appellabit, adhaerens parti, quae pro validitate agebat, cum autem in iudicio nemo unus sit, qui pro matrimonii validitate negotium insistat . . . ipse ex officio ad superiorem Iudicem provocabit." Constitution *Dei Miseratione*, §8.

[77] "Appellatione pendente vel etiam nulla . . . interposita, si ambo vel unus ex coniugibus novas nuptias celebrare ausus fuerit, volumus ac decernimus . . . praesertim ut invicem a cohabitatione separentur, quoad usque altera sententia super nullitate emanaverit . . . " Constitution *Dei Miseratione*, §9. Cf. §14, for same practice, in the Roman courts.

[78] . . . . ad officium . . . spectabit in iudicium venire quotiescumque contigerit, Matrimoniales causas supra validate vel nullitate . . . disceptari." Constitution *De Miseratione*, §6.

[79] Smith, *Eccles. Law*, II, n. 1424. Craisson, *Manuale totius Iuris*, n. 6029. Lega, *De Iudiciis Eccles.*, Vol. II, n. 361. Feije, *De Impedimentis et Dispensationibus Matrimonialibus*, n. 593.

at least to be on the safe side.[80] From the tenor of the constitution *Dei Miseratione* and from the character of subsequent responses given by the Holy See, this second view appears more likely. It was the purpose of Benedict XIV to surround marriage trials with such safeguards as would best guarantee the obtaining of the truth: the formalities of an ordinary trial would help towards this, with the carefully worded *Libellus conventionis,* the slower moving trial, checks throughout by the *Defensor*—features not required by the decretal *Saepe Contingit* of Pope Clement. Various communications sent to Bishops, soon after 1741, indicate that the Holy See so understood the purpose of Benedict XIV, i. e., that the constitution *Dei Miseratione* introduced requirements other than those mentioned specifically, the *Defensor* and the mandatory appeal.

A juridical argument, contemplated by the *pro* and *con* opinion in the Sonora case of 1848, is the following: since Benedict XIV prescribed an appeal in all marriage trials *de vinculo,* he implicitly abolished the summary trial, because mandatory appeals are against the very nature of summary procedure which proscribes unnecesary and delaying appeals.[81] To substantiate this argument, the Roman communications shall be arranged in two classes, viz., *sanationes* of faulty processes and concessions of special faculties.

2. *Sanationes of Faulty Processes.*

In connection with the *sanationes,* let it be noted that the Holy See rectified processes that were considered faulty not only because of the absence of the *Defensor* or of the second trial, but also because of other details of procedure that would not have nullified a summary procedure. In 1754, a woman had been cited for a marriage trial, but had refused both to appear and to submit questions for the witnesses; this technicality, lack of *interrogatoria,* was the basis for doubting the validity of the

---

80 Bouix, *De Iudiciis Ecclesiasticis,* II, 306.

81 S. C. C. *in Sonoren.,* 26 Aug. 1848—*Thesaurus Resol. S. C. C., t.* 108. 364-366.

process. Despite this defect, the case seemed to have been clearly proved by the answers of the witnesses to the fact proposed in the *Libellus*; for, a reference of the case to Rome, after the expiration of a two months' period of grace, brought the answer that the nullity had been established and the defect was ruled out after a consultation with the Pope.[82] A case from the diocese of *Theatine* in 1761 is important, because the cause, bigamy, was evident, the identity of the man alone having to be established. Starting in 1753, the cause was not settled till Septemer 19, 1761—due to several circumstances, one of which was the obligation of following the constitution *Dei Miseratione*. For, the Archbishop of appeal claimed that the investigations had not followed the order of the law (*haud videri factas ad formam iuris,*) especially because the *Promotor Fiscalis* had not been deputed nor had the *Defensor* been cited: in view of these defects, the Archbishop dropped the case, only to be urged again by the *actrix* to decide the question. Having been sent in this condition to Rome, the *acta* were examined and a sentence passed, favoring the nullity of the marriage, *et ad mentem*. Anxious to receive a settlement, the plaintiff again petitioned the Holy See, through the Archbishop, for a *sanatio* of the faulty process—which petition was the instruction contained in the *mens*. A simple answer, *in Decisis et amplius,* brought the case to an end. Incidentally this case illustrates the difficulties of the strict adherence to the Benedictine law, especially where the impediment was very easily established.[83] Still in the 18th century, a marriage was to be dissolved because of the impotence of the man: the latter would neither respond to the citation nor submit to

---

[82] "Nodus igitur causae est, an ex Testibus qui Judicialiter quidem, sed ad Articulos tantum, Parte non opponente interrogatoria responderunt . . . vis illata Josepho de Staso probetur; . . . Nos idem dubium subjicimus, An constet de nullitate Matrimonii in casu? Affirmative."—*Baren. Nullitatis Matrimonii,* May 14, 1754.—*Thesaurus Resol. S. C. C.,* t. 18, 25-27, 33.

[83] " . . . in compilatione processus curiae Theatinae haud deputatum vel citatum fuisse Defensorem Matrimonii." "Facta (in huius mentis executionem) per relatione S. S. ac impretata sanatione actorum in partibus gestorum contra formam Const. *Dei Miseratione,* obsequens Magdalena

an examination. An answer to the doubt thereby occasioned, was asked of the Congregation, with a plea from the *Defensores Artricis* that the process so far should not be considered null, as Marchion, the defendant, had deliberately remained away:

> ". . . voluntaria siquidem Marchionis absentia ne in ius vocaretur, iustam ei fortasse non tribuat exceptionem . . . quandoquidem retardanda non erat ob culpam Rei conventi matrimonialis causa, quae ad vitandum occasionem peccati celerem exigit expeditionem."

The Congregation answered that this physical examination should be again attempted; upon a further reply from the diocese, the Holy See accepted an informal and extrajudicial testimony to the impotence as sufficient for declaring the nullity of the marriage.[84] A peculiar case of a *sanatio* of a faulty process was decided by the Congregation for the diocese of *Codicensis,* January 24, 1857. In the first instance, the court rejected a woman's claim of "force and fear," suggesting the grounds of *ratum et non consummatum.* Having taken an appeal directly to Rome, the woman was instructed to appear before the court of the diocese of *Codicensis,* where the data for the appeal could be re-studied. Both the first trial and the action of this second instance were invalid, because several Benedictine prescriptions had not been observed, viz., no *Defensor* had been cited, no oath had been taken, the Bishop of the first court was not the competent Ordinary: in addition the proofs were not sufficient to establish force and fear or non-consummation. With good reason, the expediency of sending such imperfect *acta* on to the

---

eiusdem Constit. praecepto, denuo supplicat EE. VV. ut reassumpto enunciato Folio dignentur decernere, An sit standum vel recedendum a decisis, in casu. R. In Decisis, et amplius." S. C. C. *Theatina,* July 18 and Sept. 9, 1761—*Thesaurus Resol. S. C. C.,* t. 30, 129-132, 134. Cf. contrary decision, *in Florentina Matrimonii*—28 Jan. 1854—Pallottini, t. 13, "Matrimonium" XXVII, n. 71.

84 S. C. C. *in Ianuen. Matrim.,* 20 July 1793: 25 Jan. and 15 Mar. 1794—*Thesaurus Resol. S. C. C.,* t. 62, 184-190 and t. 63, 2, 46.

Congregation, was discussed, but the court decided on forwarding the *acta* and received the following reply: the Congregation "healed" the seriously faulty process and obtained from the Pope a dispensation *super rato et non consummato,* which was to become operative once the Bishop had proved the non-consummation to a certainty.[85] A few years later, in 1860, an appeal was taken to Rome from a court of *Perugia*: this tribunal had declared a marriage null because it had evidently been performed in fun. The proceedings of the court were null as the Vicar General who had conducted the trial, lacked jurisdiction and the *Defensor* had only appeared for half of the investigations. This twofold nullity was "healed" by the Congregation, which at the time confirmed the nullity of the marriage.[86] Such rectifying of faulty processes by the Holy See appears clearly to have been the exception and implies the obligation of the regular process: besides, the cases listed by Pallottini, all insist on the necessity of a re-hearing, in properly constituted tribunals, thereby implying the obligation of many details of ordinary trials.[87]

3. *Particular Indults.*

Through the years following the publication of *Dei Miseratione* special circumstances called for special adjustments in marriage trials; in these indults, let it be noted that the Holy

85 " . . . alia exsurgebat questio incidens . . . utrum videlicet, stante nullitate processus, impetranda esset gratia sanationis a Summo Pontifice: an potius denuo instauranda esset instructio processus iuris ordine servato." "His mature perpensis, Sacra Congregatio, praevia sanatione processus, censuit, consulendum esse Sanctissimo pro dispensatione a Matrimonio rato non consummato, sed quoad eius executionem mandavit, ut committeretur Ordinario Hispalensi in forma commissoria . . . " S. C. C. *in Codicen Matrim.*, Jan. 24, 1857—Pallottini, t. 13, "Matrimonium, §XXVII, nn. 79-83.

86 "His utrisque perpensis, cum patula omnino esset nullitas Matrimonii, Sacra Congreg.huiusmodi quidem nullitatem declaravit, sed praevia sanatione supra actorum processu, facto verbo cum Sanctissimo." S. C. C. *in Perusina Matrim.*, July 7, 1860.—Pallottini, t. 13, "Matrimonium," §XXVII, nn. 86-88.

87 Pallottini, t. 13, "Matrimonium," § XXVII, nn. 53-70.

See granted permission to proceed *summario modo,* thus revealing that it considered the Clementine summary process to have been abrogated, else there would not have been the need of such indults. In 1787, the Congregation of the Council instructed a Bishop to follow the constitution *Dei Miseratione* in gathering the materials for a declaration *super rato non consummato*: the Ordinary replied that this was practically impossible as the man, wha had married the plaintiff by proxy, but never visited her, was in some unknown city of America; in view of this, the *actrix* Rosa begged for a relaxation of the prescriptions and the Bishop added his question: "*An consulendum Sanctissimum pro dispensatione in matrimonio rato et non consummato.*" With the answer, "*Affirmative, attentis faculatibus,*" the Congregation seems to have also granted the petition of Rosa: not satisfied the Bishop asked: "*An sit standum vel recedendum a decisis...*" and was instructed to submit the case again: "*Iterum proponatur.*" A month later the final answer was sent, admitting the dispensation and again, not requiring the correction of the invalid *acta.*[88]

Under Pius VI, an unusual indult was granted to the Bishop of Agria: unusual, because it was only fifty years after the constitution *Dei Miseratione* and because its concessions practically nullified that Benedictine constitution. Wondering in what way he could accept divorce decisions of non-ecclesiastical courts, when the parties wished to re-marry, this Bishop sought an answer from the Congregation of the Inquisition (Holy Office). After recalling that such civil sentences are void (*nullius roboris ac momenti esse*) the Holy Office (August 28, 1794) admitted that the findings of such tribunals could be used as extrajudicial proof, as long as the Church courts made a new investigation of each case. Then a quinquennial faculty was granted to the Bishop empowering him to proceed summarily in the investigation of these cases, on the condition that the ordinary trial could not conveniently be held (*procedendi summarie instituto*

88 S. C. C. *in Satandren.,* April 26, July 12 and Aug. 30, 1788—Pallottini, t. 7, "*Dispensatio,*" § XII, nn. 173-176.

iudicio . . . quoties alter fieri nequeat). Even as in our canonical summary process, so by this old indult, the *Defensor* had to be cited and had to appear for the investigation;[89] in this grant it should be noted that there is not a question of an administrative process, but of a real trial, in a shortened form. Because he did not understand the precise meaning of this shortened trial, the Bishop wrote again to the Congregation, complaining in the same letter that a five year limit was a curtailment on the powers that belonged to every Bishop ("*. . . declaretur causa, ob quam, dum omnes locorum Ordinarii facultates habeat nativas iudicandi . . . facultas isthaec ei coangustiatur ad quinquennium duntaxat*"). There is a certain irony in part of the reply of the Holy Office, in 1795, whilst the meaning of a summary trial is also clearly stated. For, having repeated the Benedictine prescriptions in great detail, the Holy Office remarked:

> En quomodo, iuxta Apostolicas sanctiones, quilibet Ordinarius facultatem nativam habet iudicandi in hisce causis matrimonialibus! . . . Cum igitur haec facultas egrediatur limites ordinariae episcopalis jurisdictionis mirum non est, si ad quinquennium duntaxat coercita sit . . .

Since such requirements were ordinarily to be observed by all Bishops, any departure from them must be concessions and not a restriction (*ampliatas fuisse faculates*). This concession did not permit proceedings without the presence of the *Defensor*: regardless of how the judicial order was pared down, even to the omission of the citation and extrajudicial interrogation of the other spouse, the *Defensor* must always be on hand, as essential to the very substance of a trial. Lastly, the mandatory Benedictine appeal, to be taken after a first sentence in favor of nullity, could be omitted if the Bishop believed that the nullity

---

89 Roskovany, *Matrimonium in Ecclesia Catholica*, I, 295-297: *Monumentum*, n. 94.

had been proved, this, even if the *Defensor* favored the appeal.[90] If compared with the shortened process of canons 1990-1992, this 150 year old faculty shows these differences: it could only be used when the ordinary trial was difficult or deemed imprudent: there were no limitations as to the nature of cases to be thus summarily tried and finally, the *Defensor* was powerless to place an appeal regardless of his convictions, if the Bishop passed a definitive sentence.

Evidence of a divergent discipline in the years following the constitution *Dei Miseratione* is seen in the quinquennial faculty granted to the Archbishop of Mayence on October 8, 1803. The same problem confronted this Bavarian Prelate, as had confronted the Bishop of Agria, viz., what treatment should be accorded the decisions of civil tribunals, dissolving marriages to which baptized Protestants had been parties: especially since these Protestants, when about to remarry wth Catholics, came to feel that the civil sentences were useless in the mind of the *auctoriate matrimonium solvere.*) Pope Pius VII in his reply, condemned mixed marriages recalling to the Archbishop the tradition of the Church regarding such *connubia illicita, perniciosa et detestabilia.* In treating these marriage questions, the Archbishop was instructed to give no recognition at all to the civil decisions, even though this ran directly against the edict of the Elector of Bavaria, published in November of the previous year (*sententias huiusmodi contemni ac reiici omnino*

---

90 " . . . indultum ei fuit, ut ob expressas circumstantias valeat recedere ab enunciata tessera, modo tamen servet quod . . . ad substantiam pertinet horum judiciorum, nempe ut, quomodolibet posthabito judiciali ordine et forma, omissa quoque, si prudentia aut necessitas exigat, citatione seu extrajudiciali interpellatione alterius conjugis, non omittatur saltem deputatio probi hominis . . . qui . . . validitatem pro viribus et quantum honeste fieri potest protueatur, omnia, quae in id conferunt, diligenter persequatur, eidemque Episcopo ingenue aperiat; quodsi haud obstante hoc defensoris opere Episcopus credat matrimonium ei exhibitum esse nullum, possit remota appellatione ad solutionem procedere . . . "— Roskovany, *Matrimonium in Ecclesia Catholica,* I, 297-298: *Monumentum,* n. 95.

debere) : rather, a completely new trial was to be instituted according to the Benedictine prescriptions for every case. But if circumstances did not permit this formal trial, the Pope empowered the Archbishop with a quinquennial faculty of proceeding informally, as long as the *Defensor* was always present: the Primate could in turn delegate the same faculty to his Suffragans, when they were placed in similar straits. It is remarkable that this faculty permitted the Bishops to neglect every judicial proceeding, save the *Defensor,* as long as they arrived at certainty, using extrajudicial proof. Lastly, an appeal from a judgment of nullity had always to be taken—the Pope following the strict order of the constitution *Dei Miseratione* in this detail, and establishing a rule ordinarily foreign to summary trials. Both the faculty granted to the Bishop of Agria and this present one admitted the possibility of neglect of every sign of a judicial procsss, save the "substance," i. e., the presence of the *Defensor vinculi.* In passing, let it be noted that this faculty was more general than our summary process, because it embraced all impediments and all conditions opposed to the substance of marriage.[91]

---

[91] "Quodsi non ferat id rerum temporumque conditio, facultatem tibi ac per te Episcopis suffrangeneis tuis communicandam hoc in casu ad quinquennium concedimus . . . a praedicta methodo recedendi, sub his duabus conditionibus, prima, ut numquam . . . deficiat matrimonii defensor . . . altera, ut, si acta iudiciali methodo propter horum temporum calamitates confici nequeant, extraiudicialibus saltem atque omni alio, quo fieri poterit, modo suppleatur, ita ut numquam desint clarae concludentesque rationes ad illustrandam confirmandamque rei veritatem omnino necessariae . . .probandae sunt causae . . .quaeque sunt vel impedimentum dirimens quod matrimonium praecesserit, nec dispensatione legitima fuerit relaxatum vel conditiones quae ipsius matrimonii substantiae opponuntur . . . . Neque satis praeterea esset, unius duntaxat iudicii sententia totum hoc negotium absolvere. Ex memorata enim eiusdem Benedicti 14. constitutione decretum est, post primam sententiam matrimonii nullitatem decernentem ab ipsius matrimonii defensore interponendum esse appellationem, . . . " Roskovany, *Matrimonium in Ecclesia Catholica,* I, 455-456: *Monumentum* n. 141.

4. Obligation of the *Dei Miseratione.*

As further confirmation of the abrogation of the summary trial of Clement V, several Instructions for conducting marriage trials should be mentioned. No doubt the Congregation of the Council realized the difficulties consequent on the rigorous requirements of the Benedictine Declaration: yet it refused to relax this process, but specified points that might have been vague. In introducing the new Instruction of August 22, 1840, the Congregation wrote:

> At quia saepe in hoc difficillimo processu acta minus recte et apte ad veritatem eruendam conficiebantur, a Congregatione saepius instruetiones edidit, ac normam praescripsit quam Episcopi sequerentur.[92]

Far from replacing the constitution *Dei Miseratione,* this new instruction on marriage trials was supplementary, nor in any way did it approve a summary trial: " . . . *processus acta . . . iuxta ss. Canones, citatam s. m. Bened. VIV Constitutionem et praesentem instructionem sunt efformanda.*"[93] Likewise, the two Instructions of 1883, sent to the Oriental Bishops and to those of the United States, are not relaxations of previous legislation, they are rather a clearer determination of the details of marriage trials: in the words of the Baltimore Council, "In agendis hisce casibus pro rei gravitate exacte servetur *tum* Const. Bened. XIV . . . *tum* Instructio a S. Conger.. de Prop. Fide Nobis Communicata quae incipit 'Causae Matrimoniales'."[94]

With this point established, viz., the abolition of the older summary process, the insistence of the Holy See on the observance of the regulations of the constitution *Dei Miseratione* takes on greater importance; the Sacred Congregation of the Council was com-

---

92 Instructio, *Cum moneat Glossa.—Fontes,* n. 4069.

93 Instructio, *Cum moneat Glossa.—Fontes,* n. 4069.

94 *Acta et Decreta Concilli Plenarii Baltimorensis Tertii,* n. 304. For the Oriental Church: cf. *Instructio S. C. S. Off. ad Epis. Rituum Orient.,* a 1883—*Fontes,* n. 1076. For the United States: cf.*Instructio Causae Matrimoniales—Acta et . . . Baltim.,* p. 262 ff.

bating centuries of summary or even negligent treatment of mar riage causes and had to insist repeatedly on the new order.[95] This attitude had been already voiced by Benedict XIV in his constitution; this abolished every other custom, universal or local, whether followed wilfully or in ignorance. To follow such contrary customs would render the proceedings "Null and useless,"—a prohibition applying to every judge whether a Cardinal in Rome or a Bishop in the farthest diocese.[96] Two responses treating contrary customs specifically, may well be quoted here. In the courts of Palermo, both the ecclesiastical and the civil or regal, there was a custom of having the *Promotor Fiscalis* act as *Defensor*. An appeal to Rome brought the reply that the the *Defensor* was to be cited and that the proceedings remained null despite the custom.[97]

There is the case from the diocese of Sonora, in Mexico, decided by the Congregation of the Council, August 28, 1848. It was especially to obtain a relaxation of the necessity of a second confirmatory sentence of nullity, that the Bishop presented his petition. His request was not for a particular dispensation, but for one that would free him from the mandatory eppeal in *all* clear and evident cases ("......*in quibus aperta et notoria sit matrimonii nullitas*"), because the delays consequent upon appeals in such circumstances were so useless and so fraught with spiritual hazards. Although other requests had been conceded before, still the Bishop did not receive the faculty sought; pos-

95 Cf. the list of 25 responses in Pallottini, t. 13, "Matrimonium," tit. 17, n. 102. For earlier decisions: Rota in *Posnanien.*, 9 Mart. 1759; Rota in *Gesnen.*, 16 Mart. 1772; S. C. C. *in Corduben. Dispensatione*, 20 Sept. and 22 Nov. 1760; S. C. C. *in Albintimilliem.*, 17 Feb. 1768—from Acta of *in Panormitana*, 25 Jan. 1817—*Thesaurus Resol. S. C. C.*, t. 77, 2-6.

96 Constitution *Dei Miseratione*, 16. Cf. Constitution *Etsi Matrimonialis*, 27 Sept. 1755—*Omnia Opera Benedicti XIV*, t. 17, v. II, 288-289, 2.

97 " . . . quin huic nullitati medelam afferri possit, quod ex Regio iussu compilata sint acta iuxta ritum illius Regni . . . vel quod usus inoleverit in Panormitana Ecclesiastica Curia ita conficiendi processus" (i. e., substitution of the *Promotor Fiscalis* for the *Defensor*)—S. C. C. *in Panormitana*, 25 Jan. 1817—*Thesaurus Resol. S. C. C.*, t. 77, 2-6

sibly because this matter received greater discussion; e. g., a number of detailed *pro* and *con* arguments regarding the advisability of relaxing the Benedictine prescriptions, can still be read in the *folium* of this case. To avoid some of the delays caused by the great distances between the courts of first and second instances, the Bishop was authorized, by a special rescript, to place the appeal in some neighboring curia instead of in the distant metropolitan curia or even to accept this second trial himself, as long as a different set of priests assisted him in the hearing—and this was the only concession that he received.[98] The Benedictine rules had not been put into practice in Murienne, and one of its Bishops asked the Congregation whether two conformable sentences were required before the parties were free to marry. "Petitur an tolerari possit consuetudo permittendi novas Nuptias post unam sententiam an vero necesse sit praedictae Constitutioni simpliciter stare? . . . R. Servandam esse Const. Benedicti XIV."[99]

For the reasons outlined above, it is fairly well established that the ordinary or solemn trial was the rule for matrimonial causes after 1741; it is also easier to understand the existence of desires for shortened trials that became more frequent throughout the 19th century.

---

98 " . . . postulo itaque Sacra Congregatione declarari praedictam Const. Benedicti XIV locum non habere in casibus ita certis et notoriis ut matrimonii nullitas nulla tergiversatione celari; aut, si super hac re existit Congregationis declaratio, talis declarationis mihi copiam praebere." R. "An et quomodo annuendum sit precibus Episcopi sonorensis in casu." "Negative et ad mentem." S. C. C. *in Sonora,* August 28, 1848—*Thesaurus Resol. S. C. C.,* t. 108 (1848), 362-367. "Mens ea fertur fuisse ut peteretur a SSmo indultum quo concederetur . . . facultas committendi secundam sententiam conformem Episcopo alicui vicino, spectata distantia Metropolitani, vel sibi reservandi secundam dare sententiam cum assistentia aliquorum sacerdotum qui non habuerint partes in prima sententia."—Feije, *De Impedimentis* (3 ed. Louvain, 1885), 485.

99 S. C. C. *in Maurianem,* 15 Dec. 1877—*NRT,* XX (1888), 613.

CHAPTER II

MODERN BASIS OF THE SUMMARY MARRIAGE TRIAL (1889-1918)

Article I. Indults and Interpretations Immediately Preceding the General Interpretation of 1889

With a closer approach to the introduction of the official summary process of 1889, responses are found that permit even greater departures from the constitution *Dei Miseratione.* Some of the concessions are quite particular, for single cases; others more general, applicable to all the cases coming before this or that Ordinary. One of these involved the undispensed impediment of consanguinity; after having received a civil divorce, the woman was about to re-marry civilly. All preparations were completed for the wedding (*omnia sunt parata*) and there did not remain time enough to apply the Benedictine regulations in establishing that the woman was free to re-marry. In view of this necessity, Rome was asked for permission to proceed *extra-judicialiter*—apparently even to the omission of the *Defensor.* The Holy Office granted this petition, as long as the facts were clearly established by such an informal process, a complete relaxation of the Benedictine order, though restricted to a single case, and this a case of consanguinity—later to be included in the universal indult.[1]

[1] "Quare Vicarius Generalis . . . expostulat facultatem de nullitate prioris matrimonii extrajudicialiter cognoscendi, eamque pronunciandi modo de ea constet." R. "1 Feb., 1888. In Congregatione Generali habita coram . . . Cardinalibus Inquisitoribus Generalibus proposita suprascripta instantia, et praehabito voto D D Consultorum, iidem . . . rescribi mandarunt: Dummodo ex processu in Curia faciendo constet de existentia impedimenti, prout in precibus, et nullam obtentam fuisse dispensationem, permitti posse mulieri transitum ad alias nuptias."—*NRT,* XX (1888), 631.

Another particular faculty enabled a Bishop in France to proceed in a similar summary and extrajudicial manner, when a second marriage was evidently null because the man had been previously married and his first wife was still alive. The woman to this second marriage was reluctant to submit her case to the lengthy church trial, but could be persuaded to obtain the required declaration of freedom to re-marry, if the ordinary formalities and expenses were omitted. Clearly all the Benedictine prescriptions were to be passed over (*praetermissis formis const. Dei Miserat.*) so that the faculty granted on March 23, 1888, was quite remarkable, indicating that the mind of the Holy See had been changing since 1848, when only a very slight departure from the constitution *Dei Miseratione* was admitted. It should be of interest to note that the cause in this case, *ligamen,* was to be also included in the universal indult of the following year.[2]

Of the particular indults, probably the most revealing of the mind of the Holy Office, is that granted the Bishop of Angoulême, on September 5, 1888. Divorces were so rampant in France at the time, that even Catholics had been induced to believe that the sentences of civil tribunals enabled them to enter second marriages validly and lawfully. Because of this false state of mind, the faithful were little inclined to approach ecclesiastical courts, to seek the canonical declaration of freedom to re-marry, especially when the ordinary process involved so much time. The Vicar General of the Diocese petitioned a relaxation of the constitution *Dei Miseratione,* not only in cases that had been touched by civil courts, but as often as the nullity was evident ("*quando de nullitate matrimonii certo constet, ex his potissimum motivis, quia ob infaustam divortii legem . . .*"). In the concession of the faculty, the Holy Office specified six

---

[2] "Quare Vicarius generalis orator facultatem expostulat permittendi mulieri transitum ad alias nuptias, praetermissis formis Const. *Dei Miser.*" R. "Quod dummodo ex processu saltem summario et extrajudiciali constet de impedimento ligaminis, detur mulieri documentum libertatis." *NRT,* XX (1888), 632.

impediments that could be reviewed summarily, whenever their existence and no dispensation nor *sanatio* of them could be surely demonstrated by authentic documents or fit witnesses. This summary treatment freed from the mandatory appeal and other rules of procedure, but not from the necessity of the *Defensor.* The six impediments were the same as those in the list of June 5, 1889, but did not include Orders and Solemn Vow of Chastity as in canon 1990: lack of the canonical form was then included, whereas to-day a really informal process suffices;[3] the proofs were the same as in the universal indult of 1889—documents and other arguments. Whether other similar concessions were made previous to 1888, remains the secret of ecclesiastical archives: till earlier indults covering the same cases are revealed, this faculty of September 5, 1888, should be looked upon as the oldest, though only a particular expression of our present law.[4]

So far only indults or particular faculties had been granted by the Holy See, faculties which presupposed that the constitution *Dei Miseratione* still held *per se,* so that the rescripts were but derogations from the common law. It is now to be seen that the Holy Office approached the task of interpreting the constitution *Dei Miseratione*, by accepting and resolving doubts that

---

[3] Pont. Commis. 16 Oct. 1919, ad lum—*AAS,* X (1919), 479.

[4] "Feria IV, 5 Sept. 1888. Dummodo agatur de impedimentis consanguinitatis, affinitatis ex copula licita, cognationis spiritualis, ligaminis, disparitatis cultus (dummodo non agatur de valore baptismi forsitan collati, quo in casu semper recurrendum erit ad Sanctam Sedem), et clandestinitatis, atque ex authenticis documentis vel ex testibus fide dignis certo omnino constet de existentia impedimenti, et de dispensatione aut sanatione super eo non concessa, supplicandum Sanctissimo pro facultati procedendi ad sententiam definitivam absque appellatione, non servata forma Benedictinae Constitutionis *Dei Miseratione,* adhibito tamen et audito in singulis casibus matrimonialis vinculi Defensore.

Eadem die et feria.

Facta de his omnibus Smo. D. N. Leoni PP. XIII relatione, Eadem Sanctitas Sua resolutionem Emmum. Patrum approvabit et benigne concessit petitam facultatem."—*NRT,* XX (1888), 632-634. *NRT,* XXVI (1894), 26-28.

touched the meaning of that document. Only a few months after the Angoulême indult, the first of those doubts was settled for the Bishop of Fort Wayne, March 20, 1889. Non-Catholics wishing to join the Church in the United States were represented as having frequently been divorced civilly and remarried or at least, they desired to re-marry. To aid these converts, the Fort Wayne Bishop wished to test the validity of their previous unions, with the least possible delay and hardship. Accordingly, this Ordinary asked the Holy See if the appeal and judgment in the second instance were required, when the nullity had been clearly established because of *ligamen* or disparity of cult. His petition evidently presupposed the following of the judicial order in the first instance; yet, the Holy Office solved the doubt in a broad manner, requiring only an extrajudicial process and embracing *any* diriment impediment, not only *ligamen* or disparity of cult as in the Bishop's petition.[5]

From this response of the Holy Office, an administrative process would seem to have been sufficient: yet this was denied, not directly, but with more force, indirectly, on June 10, 1896. In its reply to the Bishop of Albany, the Holy Office admitted that it was possible to proceed summarily and extrajudicially in questions of disparity of cult and recalled this present answer to the Bishop of Fort Wayne as a statement of this law: then the Holy Office immediately added that the *forma iudicii* was always required along with the intervention of the *Defensor*.[6] How the

---

[5] "Posito tamen quod ex documentis et probationibus certis a curia episcopali et a defensore matrimonii admissis, constet primum matrimonium vel propter bigamiam alterius partis vel propter cultus disparitatem fuisse certe nullum, requiriturne appellatio defensoris et iudicium in secunda instantia . . .?" R. "Dummodo per processum saltem extrajudicialem certo constet de nullitate matrimonii ob praeexistens dirimens impedimentum evidenter comprobatum, negative." S. C. S. Off., *in Wayne-Castrensem.*—*ASS,* XXII (1893-1894), 638.

[6] ". . . licet, uti iam ab anno 1889 sub die 20 Martii . . . statuit haec ipsa S. Officii Congregatio, procedi possit praetermissis solemnitatibus in constitutione *Dei Miseratione* requisitis, modo summario et extrajudicialiter; semper tamen forma iudicialis quoad substantialia servari debet, cum

clauses of this response can be reconciled will be seen in the analysis of the general interpretation of the constitution *Dei Miseratione* to follow.

ARTICLE II. THE GENERAL INTERPRETATION OF JUNE 5, 1889.

1. *Contents*

Although the Fort Wayne answer could have been used by any Bishop in similar circumstances,[7] the Cardinal Archbishop of Paris saw fit to ask whether that answer could be used for similar cases (*norma in processibus similibus*). It was the reply of the Holy Office to this doubt, that constituted the interpretation of the constitution *Dei Miseratione* for the whole Church.[8] Using practically the same words, as in the Angoulême indult

---

interventu defensoris vinculi matrimonii . . . Planum est ex eis deducere quod semper requiritur forma iudicii quoad substantialia, necnon interventus defensoris . . ." S.C.S. Off., 10 June 1896—*Fontes*, n. 1180.

[7] This is presupposed in the reply of the Holy Office to the Bishop of Albany: ". . . licet, uti, iam ab anno 1889 sub die 20 Martii . . . statuit haec . . . congregatio procedi possit modo summario et extrajudicialiter." "Cette response . . . en effet, est la solution d'un doute, qui peut se rencontrer ailleurs que dans le territoire soumis a la juridiction de l'Eveque de Fort-Waine, . . .: C'est donc une reponse applicable dans tous les ces semblables; du moins il faudrait, nous semble-t-il, faire violence au texte pour y voir autre chose."—*NRT*, XXVI (1894), 29.

[8] "Quando agitur de impedimento disparitatis cultus, et evidenter constat unam partem esse baptizatam, et alteram non fuisse baptizatam; quando agitur de impedimento ligaminis, et certo constat primum coniugem esse legitimum et adhuc vivere; quando denique agitur de concanguinitate aut affinitate ex copula licita, aut etiam de cognatione spirituali, vel de impedimento clandestinitatis in locis ubi decretum Trident. *Tametsi* publicatum est, vel uti tale diu observatur, dummodo ex certo et authentico documento, vel, in huius defectu, ex certis argumentis evidenter constet de existentia huiusmodi impedimentorum super quibus Ecclesiae auctoritate dispensatum non fuerit; hisce in casibus praetermissis solemnitatibus in Constitutione Apostolica *Dei miseratione* requisitis, matrimonium poterit ab Ordinariis declarari nullum, cum interventu tamen defensoris vinculi matrimonialis, quin opus sit secunda sententia."—S.C.S. Off., 5 Jun. 1889—*Fontes*, n. 1118.

of 1888, the Cardinals specified a list of six impediments which could be discussed without the solemnities of the constitution *Dei Miseratione,* even to the omission of the second trial, as long as the *Defensor* was on hand. The proofs required were authentic documents or other certain arguments—not to the exclusion of witnesses—that demonstrated the existence of these impediments and the absence of any dispensation. This interpretation covered the same situations as the Angoulême indult, although with greater details, differing only in this important feature, i. e., that it was applicable to the whole Church, because it was not an indult, but a resolution of a doubt regarding the operation of the constitution *Dei Miseratione.*[9]

2. *Nature of Process*

Since this decree so closely resembles the Code legislation of Canons 1990-1992, it is deserving of more minute study. Only one trial was required under the conditions of this general declaration for the parties to be declared free from the first marriage; the mandatory appeal of the *Dei Miseratione* was clearly abrogated in the cases specified by the Holy Office. Leading authors seem to see a mere liberation from the second trial as the only concession of this 1889 decree with the obligation of a full, formal judicial process in the first instance.[10] It is believed that this opinion is not to be accepted, but rather that the first instance was to be conducted in a summary manner, shorn of customary juridical forms. This second opinion is established upon examination of a dilemma: viz., the constitution *Dei*

---

[9] S.C.S. Off., 14 Feb. 1894—*Fontes,* n. 1168. Among the *dubia* proposed to the Holy Office by the Archbishop of Warsaw, on Jan. 17, 1894, was one asking whether the response of June 5, 1889 applied to the universal Church; this *dubium* was recast, answered affirmatively and on Feb. 16 was sent to the Congreg. of the Council for publication. "An decretum S. O. 5 Junii 1889 quo in nonnullis casibus matrimonialibus derogatur solemnitatibus const. Benedictinae, sit generale, necne?" R. "Affirmative." Cf. *supra,* footnote n. 7.

[10] Gasparri, *De Matrimonio* (3 ed. 1904), II, n. 1283. Wernz-Vidal, *Ius Canonicum,* V, n. 704.

Miseratione either left Clement V's summary process untouched or it abolished this former order; if the first horn of this proposition were true, the summary marriage trial would have continued in use down to 1889 and thereafter, since no new obligations are introduced by the decree of 1889; if the second horn be true (as has been demonstrated in the previous chapter), the constitution *Dei Miseratione* was the cause of the abolition of the summary process and when the decree of 1889 in turn abolished all the rules of the constitution *Dei Miseratione*, the summary process was revived. It is clear that all the regulations of Benedict XIV's constitution were abolished, because the words, *praetermissis solemnitatibus in Const. Dei. Miser.*, are in the plural and are disjoined from the phrase, *quin opus sit secunda sententia,* which refers to one particular of the *Dei Miseratione.* No doubt it would be a stronger case if the word *extrajudicialiter* appeared in the decree, for this would refer to a summary, if not administrative proceeding; almost of equal importance, however, is the use of this word in a response to the Bishop of Albany, June 10, 1896. His request hinged on the possibility of investigating the impediment of disparity of cult not only summarily but also extrajudicially, so that, e. g., persons, even lay, could take active part as *auditores*, in the hearing, without delegation. The Holy Office admitted that such a process, summary and extrajudicial, was sufficient *even as it had been since* 1889, both before a marriage had been contracted (the *praevia investigatio* of canon 1020§1) and after the marriage ceremony, as long as in the latter case the form of a trial, in substantial points, was also observed.[11] By *modo summario* must be understood, at least, the liberation

[11] ". . . licet, uti iam ab anno 1889 sub die 20 Martii et iterum sub die 5 Junii statuit haec ipsa S. Officii Congregatio, procedi possit praetermissis solemnitatibus in Const. *Dei Miser.* requisitis, modo summario et extrajudicialiter; semper tamen forma iudicialis quoad substantialia servari debet, cum interventu defensoris vinculi matrimonii . . . quod profecto praestari a nemine poterit, nisi prius habita speciali et regulari delegatione."—S.C.S. Off. *Albanen. in America,* 10 Jun. 1896—*Fontes,* n. 1180.

from the second trial: with the addition of *extrajudicialiter,* the process in that first instance must have been somehow affected and in a word, it could be said, that the first trial was to be conducted informally, with simplicity, omitting most of those features of a regular process that would ordinarily have to be observed. If such a simplified process was the meaning of the Holy See in what way could the *forma iudicii* have been observed? The answer is found in the same reply of the Holy Office: just the barest essentials of a judicial trial were to be observed, essentials that would not have interfered with the simplicity of this quasi-administrative proceeding. Ordinarily these essentials would have been the presentation of the *Libellus,* the delegation of the *Defensor* and notary and other necessary agents and the citation of the parties; for the rest, the investigation could have proceeded without the formalities of a trial, e. g., without the stiff or rigid presentation of questions. This process would then have been judicial by nature, but quite summary in its proceedings, so that it may be called the summary judicial process.[12] Another confirmation of the summary character of the first instance is found in a Rota decision of 1912: the Rota refused to declare invalid two sentences favoring the nullity of a marriage; an exception had been placed because the two trials had been conducted *summario ritu,* whereas "they should have followed the *forma ordinaria*". The Rota explained that this exception could not be sustained since Clement's *Dispendiosam* explicitly includes marriage causes and since it was customary to treat these causes summarily; let it be noted that the Rota does not refer to the 1889 interpretation as well it might have, if the decree required the solemn trial in the first instance.[13]

---

[12] Kay, *Competence in Matrimonial Procedure,* 126; Wernz, *Ius Decretalium* (ed. altera, 1905) IV, n. 747, note 88; Triebs, "Actio ex cc. 1990-1992 Iudicialis Probatur," *Periodica,* XX (1931), 105*-107.*

[13] "Quare admitti nequit exceptio. Nam ius expresse concedebat ipsi ut sua causa summarie tracteretur, quinimo ea consuetudine nonnisi summarie hae causae in Curiis agitantur."—S. R. Rotae in Causa 31 Aug. 1912—*S. Romanae Rotae Decisiones seu Sententiae,* IV, Dec. 37, n. 2.

The judicial character of this reply of 1889 is taken for granted in other replies of Rome; e. g., in the remarks in the declaration of 1894 that the decree of 1889 applied to judicial procedure all over the Catholic world (*ita ut liceat penes omnes ... episcopales in praxi iudiciali aliquid praetermittere ...*);[14] in the reiteration by the Holy Office in 1901, of the use of the decree of 1889 in all evident cases of clandestinity, with the warning that in doubtful cases, the *Defensor* had to move a second instance, thereby supposing a judicial first instance.[15] "The history of [this] . . . procedure thwarts any attempt to project the opinion that administrative power is fundamentally operative",[16] although it was practically administrative in the simplicity of its proceedings. Thus the procedure stood till the Code: statements of pre-Code authors that "no trial is required in these excepted cases" are to be understood in this same sense, i. e., that the proceedings had not to follow the order of a regular trial and that so little of the judicial requirements were observed that the procedure could hardly be called a trial; yet under all, was an exercise of judicial power.

ARTICLE III. THE TRIAL OF CLANDESTINE MARRIAGES

Among the impediments enumerated by the Holy Office in this 1889 Decree was "clandestinity," or the failure of the parties to observe the prescribed canonical form: if this impediment could be proved clearly by documents or otherwise, the summary judicial process was to be followed. In this connection, there is a separate development both before and after 1889.

As early as 1853, special attention was given to the type of process required, in declaring the nullity of clandestine marriages. In that year the Official of the diocese of Treves remarked the hardships involved in observing the Benedictine prescriptions in such marriages and asked the Congregation of the Coun-

---

[14] S. C. Concilii, 16 Jun. 1894—*ASS,* XXVII (1894-1895), 153.

[15] ". . . quae certitudo si desit, a defensore vinculi matrimonialis ad secundam instantiam procedendum erit."—*Fontes,* n. 1251.

[16] Kay, *Competence in Matrimonial Procedure,* 125.

cil whether the constitution *Dei Miseratione* may be dispensed with when the canonical form had been neglected.[17] The reply of January 25, 1853, was: "*In casu prout proponitur, negative.*" Behind this answer is a complex history that involved various dispensations for certain parts of Germany and the doubt about publication of the decree *Tametsi* in this or that parish of Germany and the communication of exemption to the Catholic party by one freed from the form: due to such uncertainty in that section of Germany, Rome did not consider the nullity very evident and so required the formalities of a regular trial. However, from the wording of the discussion in the *Folium,* it appears that the solemnities of the Benedictine constitution could have been omitted with no obligation of a judicial process in the first instance or of a confirmatory sentence, whenever the clandestinity was notorious and without any possibility of being doubted.[18]

It has been seen that this impediment of clandestinity, when evident in existence and in lack of dispensation, was numbered in the list of the Angoulême indult of 1888 and of the general interpretation of 1889. Thereafter it was in a most summary way that such clandestinity was to be discussed, although the discussion required the *forma iudicii,* whilst the implication of the earlier Treves case was to exempt from any appearance of a judgment (*absque iudicii forma*).

---

[17] "Utrum nimirum sa. me. Bened. XIV. Const. *Dei Miseratione* . . . etiam quoad illas nuptias sit servanda quae per se pro ecclesiasticis matrimoniis nullo pacto haberi quent, ex eo quod neque in facie Ecclesiae, neque in alia in foro Ecclesiae quomodocumque valida forma contractae fuere." S.C.C. *in Trevirensi—Thesaurus Resol. S.C.C.,* t. 112 (1853).

[18] "Videant igitur Emi.P.P. an distinctio forsan adhibenda sit inter casus qui suapte natura solummodo declarationem absque iudicii forma requirant, et eos qui, ob facti vel juris quomodocumque controversiam, ad actus vere judiciales judicisque sententiam deveniant:" *discursus secretarii;* the Fathers of the Congregation then made this advised distinction. S.C.C. *in Trevirensi—Thesaurus Resol. S.C.C.,* t. 112 (1853). Cf. Feije, *De Impedimentis et Dispensationibus Matrim.,* n. 592 ad finem; *NRT,* XX (1888), 618-621.

Two years later, in 1891, the Cardinal-Archbishop of Cologne proposed a twofold doubt to Rome, which showed that he either had not heard of the 1889 declaration or doubted about its application to mixed marriages. For, his second doubt which touches the matter at hand, questioned how a summary process could be used in the trial of civil marriages of Catholics with non-Catholics. In its response of July 2, 1892, the Holy Office did not refer to the general declaration of 1889, but granted a quinquennial faculty of proceeding extrajudicially, with the intervention of the *Defensor.* This official was to act according to the rules of his office (*ad tramites iuris*) and so it seems that a second sentence was required, as this was one of the rules for the *Defensor*;[19] and this because of the special difficulties in mixed-religion, civil marriages; these same difficulties probably explain why only a five-year faculty was granted, despite the existence of a general law that covered ordinary cases of clandestinity.[20]

A last response before the Code, concerning cases involving clandestinity, is that of the Holy Office, given March 27, 1901, to four doubts proposed by several French Bishops. These doubts were concerned with various species of clandestinity, viz., vitiated form due to the presence of a priest who was not the proper pastor, attempt to escape the law by going to a place not bound by the Tridentine form and this, *in legis fraudem* or a marriage was celebrated before a non-Catholic minister or civil magistrate; in such cases, the questions ran, could a summary process, without an appeal, be used? The Holy Office merely recalled the decree of 1889, noting that it could be used

---

[19] *NRT,* XXVI (1894), 36.

[20] "2° Qua summaria ratione idem processus instrui valeat praeter normas in Benedictina Const. praestitutas?" "Ad II Supplicandum SSmo pro gratia ad quinquennium, dummodo numquam deficiat matrimonii defensor, qui munere fungatur ad tramites iuris, et extrajudicialibus saltem actis atque omni alio quo fieri poterit modo suppleatur, ut ita numquam desint clarae concludentesque probationes."—*NRT,* XXVI (1894), 23-24.

as often as the impediment was clearly proved: thereby, leaving the individual cases to the judgment of the Ordinaries.[21]

There is no reason to admit a change under the decree *Ne Temere,* in the declaration of nullity because of clandestinity. As long as the impediment was evident—a more easily established fact, because it was practically the question, whether the parties had married before a pastor within the limits of his parish or not—the same summary judicial process of 1889 could have been employed. Thus the practice stood, till the Code omitted questions of the lack of canonical form from its special marriage process of canon 1990-1992.

Briefly recounted, this historical survey reveals that the constitution *Dei Miseratione* in 1741 abrogated the summary marriage trial sanctioned in 1312 by Pope Clement V; after 1741, the full, formal trial with the mandatory appeal was the rule for all marriage causes; nevertheless, dating practically from the constitution *Dei Miseratione,* there was a trend toward simplification of the procedure evidenced in the rectifying of faulty processes and in the granting of indults; this trend was officially recognized in 1889 by the sanction of a summary marriage trial in certain cases, a trial that was not subject to the mandatory appeal nor to many of processual rules in the first instance. This trend towards simplification is further recognized in the Code which, it seems, has allowed an administrative procedure for certain marriage cases of evident nullity; in the following chapters this opinion and the consequent interpretation of the canons will be presented.

---

[21] R. "Provisum per decretum S.R. et U. Inquisitionis 5 Junii 1889, quod intellegendum est tantum de causis, in quibus certo et evidenter constet de impedimentis de quibus agitur; quae certitudo si desit, a defensore vinculi matrimonialis ad secundam instantiam procedendum erit."—S.C.S. Off., 27 Mart. 1901—*Fontes,* n. 1251.

PART II

COMMENTARY ON THE LEGISLATION OF THE CODE

CHAPTER III

THE NATURE OF THE PROCESS

Following the practice that had been in use in the Church, the Code of Canon Law has provided a special, shortened process for certain matrimonial cases. Three canons (1990-1992) contain the present legislation in this matter; these canons have been placed in the Fourth Book, on Processes, under the title dealing with marriage causes. From the studies presented in the previous two chapters, it is evident that before the Code this special process was but a species of the marriage trial. Even the use of the word *extraiudicialiter* did not destroy the judicial nature of the older procedure, for the Holy Office carefully insisted that the *forma iudicialis* was to be observed in all such simple trials.[1] The wording of the present law resembles that of the older legislation rather closely so that some authors maintain that the Code has not changed the nature of the process: other changes have been introduced, they will admit, but the process itself is still judicial.[2] Whilst the arguments advanced by these authors are weighty and worthy of diligent study, still it is now proposed to demonstrate that their conclusion need not be accepted. It is claimed here that this abbreviated process, despite its judicial history, is truly administrative, not judicial.

It is well to define as far as possible just what is meant by this claim. There is no question of trying to combine a bit of each notion, judicial and administrative, so as to satisfy all opinions; nor is *modo administrativo* to be accepted to describe how expeditiously these cases are treated, with an exercise of

---

[1] Cf. *supra*, pp. 39; 43.

[2] Kay, *Competence in Matrimonial Procedure*, 129; Noval, *De Iudiciis*, n. 873; Roberti, *De Processibus*, I, 67; Triebs, "Actio ex cc. 1990-1992 Iudicialis Probatur," *Periodica*, XX (1931), 93*-107*.

judicial power. It is difficult, nevertheless, to discover a clear-cut basis for the distinction of judicial and administrative processes; for, if the agencies exercising the power be considered, exceptions can be pointed out and if the so-called processual forms be that basis, exceptions may again be indicated,[3] It is a fact, however, that the Code has true administrative, non-judicial processes[4] and special rules for them[5] and it is maintained here that the process of canons 1990-1992 belongs in this class. It is for the Bishop in his capacity of administrator, and not as judge of his diocese, to decide these cases: as administrator, he exercises a power that has been described as operating for a speedy settlement of problems for the good of souls—a power that ordinarily is not restrained by the fullness of judicial forms, although imitating these to obtain certainty.[6] If the Bishop were to settle all questions regarding marriages personally there would be no practical purpose, on this score, of resolving the dispute; but generally Bishops relinquish such cases to the judgment of others and herein lies a practical difficulty. The *Officialis* has ordinary power of judging, and is excluded from participation in the administration of the diocese, for the canon treating of his appointment (*c.*1573) ascribes to him only this judicial power: hence, in virtue of his office, he is incompetent to act in administrative processes and may not therefore decide the cases of canon 1990, in the event that these must be handled administratively. On the contrary, the Vicar-General is the Bishop's aid in governing the diocese[7] and may substitute for the Bishop in settlement of all matters, as long as the limitations of canon 368 §1 are observed and he may therefore declare the nullity of marriages, under canons 1990-1992, if these represent an administrative process.

---

[3] Roberti, *De Processibus* I, 66-67.

[4] Canons 1962-1963: 1933: 1999; 2142 ff.

[5] Canons 1061: 2146 § 1-3: 2194: 2287: Response of the *Praeses* Pont. Commis., 22 Maii 1923, ad canones 1552-1601—*AAS*, X (1924), 251.

[6] Vermeersch-Creusen, *Epitome Iuris Canonici* (1931), III, nn. 341-343.

[7] Canon 368 § 1.

The Code has different rules to regulate the proper place for settling of judicial and administrative matters (canons 201, 1560 §3 and 1964). If the process is judicial, the competence-rule of the regular marriage trial *must* be followed, with due respect to indults; thus an Ordinary would have to refuse to receive the petition of those who were married outside his diocese or when the *pars conventa* is not his subject. If the procedure is administrative, the discussion and resolution of the cases may be made, strictly speaking, even when the defendant is not a subject of that Ordinary, as long as the "actor" is a subject. This difference has been recognized and has served as the basis for dioceses to refuse or to transfer certain petitions for which they considered themselves incompetent in their view of the judicial nature of the process. It is with a view to these and other practical consequences that this dissertation seeks to establish the administrative nature of that canonical summary process used for certain marriage cases.

To prove this contention, the following will be studied in detail:

Article I. The titles and words of the canons;

Article II. Recent rescripts of the Holy See regarding canons 1990-1992;

Article III. An Instruction of the Sacred Congregation of Sacraments dealing with the Italian Concordat;

Article IV. Supplementary arguments, viz., from authority and indirect reasoning.

ARTICLE I. THE TITLES AND LANGUAGE OF THE CANONS

1. *The Titles or Inscriptions*

From the titles or captions of the Fourth Book, a certain argument for the administrative nature of the 1990 process cannot be obtained. At first glance the arrangement of this Book favors the judicial character of this shortened marriage procedure, because Chapter VII (i. e., Canons 1990-1992) is to be found in a truly judicial setting, viz., under Title XX (*De causis matri-*

monialibus) of the Second Section (*De peculiaribus normis in certis quibusdam iudiciis servandis*) of the first part (*De Iudiciis*) of Book Four. In view of the rule of Decretal law, *a rubro ad nigrum valet illatio,* one is inclined to conclude that canons 1990-1992 have been so placed because of their judicial character; yet such an inference need not always be made for there are exceptions as another old rule reveals, *nigrum latius patet rubro.* It is because of this possibility of exception, that the location of Chapter VII in a judicial surrounding need not force the conclusion of its judicial character and accordingly does not prohibit that the process of these canons is administrative. The presumption that leads to the judicial nature of these canons is false, viz., that all the matter appearing in this First Part of the Fourth Book are so intimately connected with trials as to be either real trials themselves or judicial in some way and nothing else. This presumption falls when three divisions of this First Part are examined. From the inscriptions of Section Two (*De peculiaribus normis in certis quibsdam iudiciis servandis*), one should naturally expect that all the subsequent matter would be of a strictly judicial nature and yet the very first title (XVIII) deals with a non-judicial affair, i. e., several methods of *avoiding* trials. Their connection with the whole matter of judgments evidently urged the placing of these canons (1925-1932) with the treatment on trials—so much is clear; yet their very location in this Section Two would force one to consider them as a type of a trial, if the presumption of the proponents of a judicial procedure in canons 1990-1992 were valid and evidently these methods of avoiding trials are not themselves trials.[8] Again, the following title (XIX) contains another substitution for a trial, viz., the procedure for correcting one who has committed some fault or crime (Chapter III); this is a judicial matter (*ad modum actus iudicialis*) and so has been appropriately placed with other judicial matters; it is mentioned, however, so as to point out that a title does not necessarily qualify all the matters arranged under it, i. e., in

---

[8] Roberti, *De Processibus,* I, 25.

this case the nineteenth title is "Concerning the criminal *trial,*" whilst the third chapter deals not with a trial, but with a substitution thereof.[9]

If the chapter containing canons 1990-1992 were administrative, it should appear in the third part of this Fourth Book because there are gathered the processes which have been described as administrative; such is the argument of one favoring the judicial character.[10] This view rests on another presumption that is not necessarily true, viz., all processes of like nature should be gathered by themselves: as well say that canons 1925-1932 should be removed from the Part on Trials because they present ways of settling disputes outside of trials. Likewise canons 654-668 should have been left, as in the draft of the Code presented to the Bishops in 1914, in the section dealing with Ecclesiastical Trials because these canons outline the *trial* for the dismissal of certain religious.[11] Rather the reason for the grouping of some canons of the Code is the logical connection of subject matter, e. g., trials of religious in that Part dealing with the religious and all those proceedings which represent some exception or special feature over and above the regular trial (canons 1925-1998), under a common heading (. . . *de peculiaribus normis* . . .) even though evidently they are not all trials nor of a judicial nature. Since those presumptions built upon the situation of canons in the Code need not always be urged, it is believed that the location of Chapter VII (canons 1990-1992) in a judicial setting does not forbid that this proceeding be administrative and does not therefore present an obstacle to the proof of the following articles. The caption, *de casibus exceptis,* permits the application of the note, *administrative,* to canons 1990-1992, even though they are subordinated

---

[9] "nigrum latius quam rubro:" Noval, *De Iudiciis,* p. 480. Cf. Chapter III of Title XX—a mere petition is included under a title dealing with matrimonial *causes.*

[10] Kay, *Competence in Matrimonial Procedure,* 132.

[11] Codice di Divitto Canonico, Riassunto e Dilucidazioni, *Il Monitore Ecclesiastico,* XXXIII (1921), 15.

to the various truly judicial inscriptions. The question "how can a generic word (case) coming in a subdivision restrict a specific term (cause) used in a grand division"[12] is to be answered from the arguments just presented, i. e., the Code evidently includes under the same title matters that are not, strictly speaking, divisions or species of the subject-matter of that title: it seems that an example of such an arrangement is the present chapter VII of Title XX. In this instance, a chapter is headed by a word (*casibus*) general by its nature, but the only one fit to be used of an administrative proceeding: a word that is not to be taken as a restriction of the XX title (*causis*), but as introducing a new subject connected with that title, i. e., introducing a special process to be substituted in certain cases for the regular trial. This connection is one of exception and well placed is this chapter to emphasize its exceptional character; for since the location of the chapter is not an obstacle, its caption, *casibus exceptis,* exempts it directly from the rules given in the title on matrimonial causes and indirectly from the other judicial rules presupposed in marriage trials, with due respect to the limitations given in the canons 1990-1992—limitations which although drawn from the judicial proceedings do not necessarily establish the canons as judicial inasmuch as administrative processes imitate the prescriptions of regular trials.[13] Briefly, once the administrative character of canons 1990-1992 has been established, there is no objection to be found either in the location or in the caption of these canons.

2. *The Language of the Canons*

Because the language of these canons (1990-1992) is uncertain, even ambiguous, it should not be emphasized as an argument by itself to determine the character of the power exercised. Of course, one rule of interpretation is that based on the

---

[12] Kay, *op. cit.,* 131 .

[13] This last will be dealt with more fully in a subsequent section. Cf. Vermeersch-Creusen, *Epitome,* III, n. 343. Triebs, "Actio ex cc. 1990-1992 iudicialis probatur," *Periodica,* XX (1931), 99.*

words of the law, i. e., that the meaning proper to the words in the text or context must guide the interpretation.[14] Without doubt, many of the words have a judicial sense and yet others are administrative and others, ambiguous, are open to either interpretation. When some words are indicated as ambiguous, these may be more readily considered as administrative, because the language for judicial matters is more precise, better defined than the terminology of administrative proceedings which have but few proper words (e. g., *decretum, recursus*). The presumption is that words of a general meaning are not judicial, but represent an effort to describe an administrative proceeding. It is now proposed to demonstrate that the wording of canons 1990-1992 confirms the administrative view to be established in the following articles of this chapter. Each canon will be considered in turn, with references to the others when necessary.

Canon 1990. Of the three canons, this is the most clearly administrative and deserves close study because it is the guide for the whole summary process.[15] The caption to these canons (*De casobus exceptis a regulis hucusque traditis*) may well be recalled in connection with canon 1990; it exempts from *all* the judicial rules given in the first part of Book IV. That this is the meaning of the caption is revealed by a reading; for the language is general, mentioning ''rules'' without restrictions of ''some'' or ''few'' or ''last-mentioned'': furthermore, the words *hucusque recensitis* must be accepted as referring to all the provisions for a trial, not merely to those of Title XX for marriage processes; this Title is but a supplement to the ordinary judicial regulations and implicitly includes all the ordinary regulations which are in harmony with the special rules for matrimonial causes. Hence this phrase ''rules so far recounted,'' even though it appears in a subordinate chapter, implicitly includes all the rules outlined for trials in Book IV.[16] Strictly speaking, however, this caption has not the force of law which is found in the words of the canons.

---

[14] Canon 18.

[15] Cf. can. 1992 ". . . eodem modo de quo in can. 1990. . . ."

[16] Vlaming, *Praelectiones Iuris Matrimonii,* II, n. 803.

In the canons, this interpretation of the caption finds confirmation, for the key-words (*praetermissis solemnitatibus hucusque traditis*) are again general, without any restriction, i. e., *all* "the solemnities thus far recounted" may be omitted. Besides, it was deemed necessary to mention several features, *citatis partibus*, and *defensoris vinculi interventu*, thus that *no* other formalities of the regular trial must be observed.[17] Once the meaning of *solemnities* is decided, there will be no difficulty in determining whether this or that solemnity is to be retained; *all* are to be omitted save those specified in these three canons. One author has contrasted solemnities with essential regulations, distinguishing between the accidental points (*solemnitates*) and the essential points of a trial: from this distinction he argues that the process of canons 1990-1992 is fundamentally judicial, though shorn of the customary formalities.[18] It is believed that this conclusion does not necessarily follow. No doubt, the *solemnitates iudicii* are the regulations and formalities prescribed by positive law to give form to a trial and to safeguard the acquisition of the truth[19] and as such may be dispensed with when the chances of error are remote. In the present case *all* these special regulations are to be omitted so that the procedure has been pared down to a mere skeleton: there remains only the matter to be decided, the parties, the arbiter or judge and the *Defensor vinculi*. Those favoring the judicial opinion would view these as the bare essentials of a trial (*objectum, subjectum passivum, subjectum activum, forma legitima*);[20] surely the pres-

[17] An eminent canonist would confirm this, as witness his rendering of this phrase, ". . . praetermissis cuiusque generis solemnitatibus seu quovis processu iudiciali,"—Gasparri, *De Matrimonio* (1932), II, 306. To like effect writes another in his article favoring the judicial character of canons 1990-1992: "Scilicet praecepta de processu solemni in praecedentibus titulis libri IV exposita, in his casibus exceptis non obtinent, sed omnia ad praescripta canonum 1990-1992 peraguntur." Triebs, "Actio ex cc. 1990-1992 iudicialis probatur," *Periodica*, XX (1931), 98.*

[18] Kay, *Competence in Matrimonial Procedure*, 131, 133.

[19] Lega, *De Iudiciis Ecclesiasticis*, I, 1, n. 591.

[20] Noval, *De Iudiciis*, nn. 15-16.

ence of the first three elements, viz., subject-matter, parties and arbiter, do not suffice to define a trial: these are equally the constituents of an administrative proceeding. It is only the *forma legitima* that may distinguish a trial from other non-judicial proceedings.[21] Since all other formalities are to be omitted, the *Defensor vinculi* and the citation of the parties are the only links in establishing the *forma legitima.* It is contended that the presence of the *Defensor* is not a sufficient proof for this *forma legitima,* as he is required in other proceedings which are not judicial and his presence there does not make them judicial: viz., in the informative process for a dispensation *super rato non consummato*;[22] in the settlement by a judge's decree (not by an interlocutory sentence) of incidental questions arising in marriage trials.[23] His presence is to be explained as in the *Super rato* process, viz., by reason of a special regulation due to the sacredness of the case. Likewise, citation of the parties need not characterize the proceedings as judicial. The natural law requires that the parties to a marriage be made aware of the discussion of their union, which affects themselves so vitally: to guarantee this fundamental right, the judicial system has developed the citation. It does not necessarily follow that the presence of a single judicial term makes the proceedings judicial; for administrative processes imitate trials in acquiring the truth and still remain administrative: e. g., the notary of canon 2142 and the introduction of witnesses as a special feature or concession in canon 2145 (*at duo vel tres testes*) and the provision of canon 2189 §2. The phrase *citatis partibus,* then, is directive, imitating the regular citation as a model for guaranteeing

[21] *Ibid.,* n. 23.

[22] "Inde duo consequuntur magni ponderis: primo quod huiusmodi causae, utpote quae non promoventur ab actione iudiciali contentiosa aut criminali sed ex benigna concessione Sanctae Sedis annuentis oratoris precibus, non sunt verae iudiciales, sed magis gratiosae seu administrativae."—*Regulae Servandae, In Processibus Super Matrimonio Rato et Non-Consummato,* Decretum, p. 4.

[23] Canons 1839 and 1840, § 1; cf .1709, § 3; 1856, § 2.

the presence of the parties.[24] The other words of this canon, bearing on the discussion, all favor the administrative nature of the power. *Casibus* is one of those general terms that must be used when an effort is made to describe an administrative proceeding: whilst, strictly speaking, it could be applied to a trial, this meaning is not to be accepted, for the judicial process has a proper term, *causa*. *Ordinarius* evidently could refer to the Bishop acting either in a judicial or in an administrative manner, since he has the two-fold power.[25] The word does not help in settling the dispute until the Bishop transfers these cases to another for settlement: is the *Officialis* competent by reason of canon 1573, §1 or should these matters be treated by the Vicar General? Until it is certain that the Ordinary acts as a judge in canons 1990-1992, the Code's definition of *Ordinarius* must answer the question and so it is the Vicar General who is indicated by the canon as the Bishop's substitute.[26] Since the Vicar General ordinarily lacks judicial power, it is fair to argue that the *Ordinarius* must be viewed as acting administratively in canons 1990-1992.[27] The last word to claim attention is *declarare;* this again is a general term, applicable to either type of process. It is actually used in connection with a truly judicial affair:[28] yet in the present context it is far more ambiguous than would be exercised if the process were judicial; this appears from a comparison with the termination of an ordinary marriage trial (*Quare tribunal ad definitivam sententiam ne deveniat, nisi* . . .).[29] Since the elements, remaining after the exemption from all judicial solemnities, are common to judicial and administrative proceedings, since the two judicial terms do not necessarily postulate a trial and since the other terms may be enlisted to

[24] ". . . nam praevia citatio partium pertinet ad substantiam cuiuscumque iudicii, imo et cuiuscumque arbitrii. . . ."—*Jus Pontificium*, XI (1931), 255.

[25] Canon 335, § 1.

[26] Canon 198, § 1.

[27] Canon 1573, § 1 and § 7; cf. *supra*, p. 52.

[28] Canon 1986.

[29] Canon 1984, § 2.

favor the administrative view, it is maintained that canon 1990 supports the administrative view to be established in the following article.

Canon 1991. Under certain circumstances, specified in canon 1991, the *Defensor vinculi* must submit the declaration of nullity to a revisional discussion. This action of the *Defensor* appears to be a true appeal subject to the ordinary regulations of appeals:[30] for the language describing this obligation is practically the same as that prescribing the appeal in the regular matrimonial trial (. . . *vinculi defensor . . . ad superius tribunal provocare debet.*)[31] There is this difference, however, that canon 1991 has the word *declarationem* in place of *sententiam* and strictly, an appeal is an action taken from a sentence (*Pars . . . itemque promotor iustitiae et defensor vinculi . . . ius habent a sententia appellandi*),[32] it is not maintained that this substitution of words suffices to disprove conclusively the notion of a true appeal, but it does indicate an uncertainty of language that prevents a final argument for either view. Canon 1991 appears to contain a judicial prescription and as such finds place in this administrative process in virtue of a special rule. Having in view the safeguarding of the sanctity of the marriage contract, the Code here prescribed a method proved salutary in the regular judicial procedure. If it is argued that *iudicem* of this canon supposes the judiciary department at least in the second instance and therefore a change in the character of the process from the first instance,[33] it may be replied that *iudicem* is not so strictly a judicial term as to presuppose a judicial action wherever it appears: the very definition of *decreta,* some of which are nonjudicial, includes the term *iudicis.*[34] Evidently the word *acta* can be referred to either judicial or administrative matters:[35] note that *casu* again is used in this canon.

---

[30] Connolly, *Appeals,* 68.

[31] Canon 1986.

[32] Canon 1879.

[33] Kay, *Competence in Matrimonial Procedure,* 135.

[34] Canon 1868, § 2; cf. canons 1840, § 3 and 1966.

[35] Canon 1813, § 1, 1° and 3°.

Canon 1992. The last of the three canons describes the method of reviewing the first declaration of nullity: the *judge* (who need not be a judicial personage) is to omit all solemnities in his revisional study, except the *Defensor vinculi.* The only new word to favor the judicial view is the name given the first decision, *sententia*: this cannot be urged too strongly, because in the former two canons, *declarare* and *declarationem* are used where the more precise judicial terminology of *definire* and *sententia* could have been used.[36] To confirm the administrative view, the change *casus* to *causa* should be noted: when the *judge* rejects the nullity decision of the first instance, the question regarding the validity of the bond is to be submitted to the ordinary procedure, and no longer is a *case,* but is a *cause* or matter for judicial treatment.

This study of the language of the canons shows that judicial terms may be balanced by administrative ones or understood in a non-judicial sense. In view of this uncertainty, an argument for the administrative character may not be based on the language alone: it is believed, however, that the language does not forestall an administrative understanding which will appear the more correct from the following article.

ARTICLE II. RECENT RESCRIPTS OF THE HOLY SEE REGARDING CANONS 1990-1992

In short, the argument shall run as follows: the prohibition of non-Catholics as *actores* under the date of Jan. 27, 1928, evidently refers to a judicial matter and does not admit an exception for any matrimonial cause, short of a special faculty frcm the Holy Office; yet this prohibition does not extend to the cases of canons 1990-1992; therefore these canons do not prescribe a judicial procedure.

---

[36] The argument that *declarare* has been used in canon 1990 "to show that the sentence there was *per se* definitive or final" is not to be accepted, because the same word, *declaraverit,* appears in canon 1986 describing the first of two required sentences. Kay, *op. cit.,* 135.

On the 27th of January, 1928, the Holy Office in resolving a *dubium* declared that non-Catholics as plaintiffs (*actores*) could no longer regularly introduce matrimonial causes.[37] This response clearly identified the special right of accusing the invalidity of a marriage with those rights denied to non-Catholics because of their separation from the Church; already three years before, the Holy Office had restricted the right of being *actores* to Catholics, so that in each case of a marriage between two non-Catholics, recourse had to be taken to the Holy See.[38] Undoubtedly the reply refers to the marriage trial that is indisputably judicial, viz., the regular trial of canons 1960 ff., for it is referred by all to that canon dealing with the *fitness* of the plaintiff in a marriage trial(can. 1971). Furthermore, it is in connection with matrimonial *causes* that the restriction falls on non-Catholics and of course such *causes* are matters for judicial cognition.[39] From the wording of this answer, there appears to be no provision for any cases outside of the strictly so-called matri-

---

[37] S. C. S. Off., 27 Jan. 1928—*AAS,* XX (1928), 75.

[38] In Congregatione generali S. R. et U. Inquisitionis, propositis sequentibus dubiis ab A. T. expositis, utrum nempe: 1. Tribunal ecclesiasticum iudicare possit de validitate matrimonii duorum acatholicorum, instante parte acatholica, quae nempe cum catholico contrahere vult, aut parte catholica acatholico nupturiente, aut utraque, aut solo Promotore iustitiae? 2. Quod tribunal competens sit eiusmodi causae, an loci, in quo matrimonium celebratum est, vel domicilii aut quasi-domicilii partis acatholicae, vel catholicae instantis?

Emi et Rmi Patres una mecum Inquisitores Generales respondendum mandarunt:

Ad 1. Recurrendum in singulis casibus.

Ad 2. Ut in Collectanea de Propaganda Fide (pars. II n. 2170) (June 23, 1903).

Quam Emorum Patrum resolutionem Ssmus approbare dignatus est. Et fausta cuncta atque felicia Tibi a Domino apprecor.

A. T. Revmae addictissimus.

R. Card. Merry del Val.

Illmo et Revmo D. Archiepiscopo, Friburgen.—*AfkK,* CVII (1927), 569-574.

[39] "Causa est res, seu ius deductum in iudicium"—Vives, *Compendium Iuris Canonici,* p. 409; c. 10, X, *de verb. signif.,* V, 40.

monial *causes;* at the same time, that restriction as to non-Catholic plaintiffs is to apply to *all* marriage *causes*: the Holy Office seems not to contemplate any cases that would be exempt from Its response, short of a special faculty granted by Itself. In fact, so anxious is the Holy See that non-Catholics be entirely excluded from instituting an action, that the Holy Office is reported to be unwilling to grant the permission to accept petitions dealing with marriages in which the plaintiff is the non-Catholic party, unless such a one will be first converted.[40] This rule of the Holy Office, then, applies to every judicial marriage process and is interpreted so strictly as not to admit of exceptions.

In view of this strictness, the exemption of the cases of canon 1990 from the same decree assumes peculiar importance; viz., non-Catholics may bring in these cases, without special authorization from the Holy See, for a decision under canons 1990-1992 and therefore this short process must be non-judicial.[41] By far the most important argument to establish the exemption of the summary process from this decree is drawn from some recent rescripts of the Holy Office.[42] These rescripts do not have as pur-

[40] "Oratrix convertatur et postea iterum recurrat": S. C. S. Off., 17 Julii 1928—*Theologisch-Praktische Quartalschrift,* LXXXIII (1929), 788.

[41] Gasparri, *De Matrimonio* (ed. nova), II, p. 293. Cf. V. Schaaf, O. F. M., "Competence of Ordinary in a case under Canon 1990," *Eccles. Review,* LXXXV (1931), 308, ff.: Charles E. Park, "Competence of Ordinary in a case under Canon 1990," *Eccles. Review,* LXXXVI (1932), 68-73.

[42] Petition of the Bishop of Harrisburg: . . . Nunc autem N. . . . a Curia Nostra declarationem nullitatis sui matrimonii humile petit, asserendo impedimentum dirimens disparitatis cultus tempore matrimonii contracti exsistisse. Cum vero iuxta decisionem S. C. Sancti Officii, 27 Januarii, 1928, Curiae Diocesanae ad huiusmodi causas adiudicandas incompentententes, ob inhabilitatem partium standi iudicio, declarentur, Ego, Episcopus Harrisburgi, hanc causam ad eandem S. Congregationem Sancti Officii refero.

Ex aedibus S. Officii, die 20 Aprilis, 1931: Excellentia Revma.

Litteris die 19 Septembris elapsi anni ad S. Officium datis, Excellentia Tua Revma notum faciebat acatholicam N. . . . declarationem petiisse invaliditatis matrimonii, quod ipsa contraxit cum N. . . . anno, 1917, cum asserto impedimento disparitatis cultus. Ratio hujus licentiae petendae af-

pose, the granting of a mere faculty for receiving the matrimonial cases of non-Catholics—a faculty that could have been expected in view of the special circumstances admitted by the Holy Office in 1928 (*Si quidem autem speciales occurrant rationes . . .*). Rather, these several rescripts are declarations of the meaning of the law. Evidently the Holy Office did not restrict the extent of the law; nor did it extend it because non-Catholics would enjoy all the rights consequent on baptism unless prohibited and these responses merely *declare* that non-Catholics are not prohibited from asking a pronouncement on the validity of their marriages, as outlined in canons 1990-1992. Generally speaking, private rescripts can not be extended, so as, e. g., to be used by others than the recipient; but these particular

---

ferebatur mulieris desiderium novas nuptias cum viro catholico ineundi.

Haec Suprema S. Congregatio, re diligenter considerata, respondendum mandavit, praefatum casum ab ipso Ordinario pertractari posse ad norman Canonum 1990-1992.

Horum Canonum praescripta integre et precise in re definienda erunt servanda, sive quoad certitudinem impedimenti et omissae dispensationis, sive quoad modum procedendi. Si res dubia manserit, Sancto Officio erit deferenda.

Ubi de invaliditate matrimonii in casu ex processu certe constiterit, dispensationem ab impedimento disparitatis cultus poterit Excellentia Tua ab hac S. Congregatione implorare, expositis causis quae ipsam suadeant et praehabitis cautionibus exigi solitis ad normam Canonis 1061, ut novae nuptiae cum viro catholico contrahi possint.

Maximam meam observantiam Tibi obtestor ac permaneo
Excellentiae Tuae Revmae
Addictissimus
(S.) D. Card. Sbaretti
Episcopus Sabinensis et Mandelensis
Secretarius

Petition of the Bishop of . . .

Ego . . . Ordinarius . . . humillime propono dubium sequens et quatenus responsio fiat negative, petat ut mihi vel Curiae Nostrae indultum procedendi in talibus adiunctis concedatur.

Rationes sunt:

Fere impossibile est multis causis recurrendi ad Sanctam Sedem tum quia saepe partes iam civiliter divortium acceperunt, tum quia pro dolor, iam contra praescripta ecclesiae contraxerunt cum catholicis.

rescripts are declarative, indicating in an official, though private manner what the meaning of the law is and can serve as a guide to others who are confronted by the same difficulty, without the obligation of seeking permission from the Holy See or of having a renewal of such a declaration for each diocese (canon 17 §2).

From the wording of the first petition and the response to it, non-Catholics, strictly speaking, would be admitted only to those nullity proceedings wherein disparity of cult was the grounds; however it is clear enough that non-Catholics may seek a declaration of nullity because of *other* of the impediments mentioned in canon 1990. The petition was based on disparity of cult because that was the most frequent case involving non-Catholics: furthermore neither in the canons nor in the reply of the Holy

---

In casibus ultime recensitis finis actionis est ut matrimonia, nulla propter impedimenta dirimentia declarentur nulla in ordine ad validanda matrimonia cum catholicis contracta vel contrahenda, praesertim si serius periculum defectionis ex parte catholica.

Omni, etc.,

QUAESITUM.

An RESPONSIO Sacrae Congregationis Sancti Officii, die 27a Januarii 1928, data, prohibens ne acatholicus in causis matrimonialibus *actoris* partes agere possit, comprehendat causas quae secus secundum Canonum 1990 tractentur?

Ex Aedibus S. Officii
die 14 Aprilis 1931.

Excellentia Revma,

Litteris die 14 Februarii elapsi anni ad S. Officium datis, exponebat Excellentia Tua Revma casus quosdam apud istam Revmam Curiam Episcopalem examinandos occurrere, in quibus, ad matrimonia mixta convalidanda, de valore matrimonii a parte acatholica prius initi judicium ferri oportet.

Suprema haec Sacra Congregatio, re diligenter considerata, respondendum mandavit, praefatos casos ab ipso Revmo Ordinario ad normam Canonum 1990-1992 pertractari posse, dummodo horum Canonum praescripta integre et praecise in causis definiendis serventur, sive quoad certitudinem impedimenti et omissae dispensationis, sive quoad modum procedendi.

Si res dubia manserit, ad Sanctum Officium erit deferenda.

Maximam, etc.,

D. Card. Sbarretti, . . .

Office can be found any reason for a distinction between the procedures for disparity of cult and for the other impediments: as a matter of fact the second petition and response are not restricted, even in language, to disparity of cult cases, but are quite general (. . . *nulla propter impedimenta dirimentia* . . .). And of course, the reply refers to canons 1990-1992. So it may safely be maintained that these rescripts refer to the process of canons 1990-1992 *as a whole* and not only to one of the cases there contemplated.

After this discusion, it remains only to point out that these two rescripts declare the Bishop free to receive those cases introduced by non-Catholics under canons 1990-1992 (*praefatum casum ab Ordinario pertractari posse ad normam Canonum* 1990-1992 . . .; *praefatos casus ab ipso Revmo Ordinario ad normam canonum* 1990-1992 *pertractari posse* . . .). Hence the procedure of these canons is exempt from that restriction now so stringently enforced for a judicial marriage trial, viz., the inability of non-Catholics to institute an action, and is therefore administrative. To support this contention, the careful use of words in these rescripts should be noted: both petitions sent to the Holy See asked about non-Catholics acting in the matrimonial *causes* of canons 1990-1992: the Holy Office in replying changed this language, using *casum* and *casus;* the force of this change can easily be understood in view of the administrative nature of these canons.

ARTICLE III. AN ISTRUCTION OF THE SACRED CONGREGATION OF SACRAMENTS DEALING WITH THE ITALIAN CONCORDAT

Soon after the ratification of the Concordat between the Holy See and Italy, instructions were issued to indicate the way in which this agreement was to operate. On July 8, 1929, the Sacred Congregation of Sacraments circulated its set of rules dealing with Article 34 of the Concordat, viz., the question of marriages; in the fifth chapter, the Sacred Congregation comes to speak of the mode in which the statement of the nullity of a marriage is to be recorded: copies of the decision must be sent to the Supreme Tribunal of the *Signatura* which "in turn shall communicate them to the Court of Appeal of the district to which the Commune belongs and to which had been transmitted the account of the celebration of the marriage." In passing, the Sacred Congregation describes the nature of this nullity-decision and it is this description that so confirms the conclusion of the previous article. These transcripts, sent to the *Signatura,* should contain "the provisions and the sentences of nullity of marriage rendered final (can. 1987), whether the respective causes have followed the judicial course or the administrative or economic one (can. 1990) . . ."[43]

In view of the language, there can be no question but that the Sacred Congregation has called the process of canons 1990-1992 truly administrative; evidently the word *amministrativo* is more than a mere synonym for a shortened or economic process, for the two correlative clauses introduced by *sia . . . sia* clearly mark a contrast: if the first clause describes a process that is judicial, the second evidently excludes that notion when it describes another process as administrative. No one may conclude from this remark of the Congregation that the dispute is settled; this Congregation has not been constituted the official interpreter of the Code and accordingly its statement is not final; however, it is worthy of respect and may serve as a guide until an official interpretation is issued. Coupled with the utterances of the Holy Office, studied in the previous article, this statement of the Sacred Congregation would seem to favor the administrative view.[44]

---

[43] "n. 49. I provvedimenti e le sentenze di nullita di matrimonio rese executive (can. 1987) sia che le relative cause abbiano sequito il corso giudiziario, sia quello amministrative o economico (can. 1990) . . . saranno d'ufficio trasmesse . . . dal tribunale ecclesiastico di appello . . ." S. C. de Sacram., 8 Jul. 1929—AAS., XXI (1929), 361.

[44] An Instruction of the *Signatura* on the same matter is not so telling, as it merely adopts the view-point of the Code, calling the one process *formal* and the other *exceptional*: at least this Instruction does not argue for the judicial nature of canons 1990-1992. "Le sentenze dichiaranti la nullita del matrimonio, tanto se il loro processo abbia seguito il corso for-

ARTICLE IV. SUPPLEMENTARY ARGUMENTS

In this last article are to be presented a survey of the opinions of the authors and replies to several difficulties occasioned by responses of the Holy See.

1. *Opinions of the Authors*

The number of those favoring the judicial notion are few, but worthy of study because they bring reasons to substantiate their claim. Noval admits that the process is very special, yet sees the essentials of a trial in the *interventum iudicis, auditionem litigantium, interventum defensoris, sententiam* and *appellationem;* when so arrayed, these elements are impressive but already it has been shown that they do not postulate a trial. He infers from the reply of the Pontifical Commission, stating that no judicial process is needed for lack of form-cases, that canons 1990--1992 are judicial; the inconsistency of this inference will be indicated in the second part of this article.[45] Blat clearly favors the judicial view, invoking a reply of the Holy Office (10 Jun. 1896) for support; this appeal to the pre-Code order is not convincing.[46] Roberti comes to call the process judicial when he is defining the distinction between administrative and judicial power; in a personal communication to Kay, he expressed the same conviction again, but has not advanced reasons for his view.[47] By far the most ardent advocates of the judicial opinion are Triebs and before him, Kay, who give orderly argu-

male di cui ai canoni 1960 a 1989 del *Codex iuris canonici,* quanto se siano state trattate colla procedura eccezionale ed economica di cui ai canoni 1990 a 1992, appena siano divenute definitive ed executive a norma dei canoni 1987 o 1992, saranno tranmesse . . ." *Litterae Circulares*: Supremum Signaturae Apostolicae Tribunal, Aug. 3, 1929. *Appollinaris,* II (1929), 425.

[45] Noval, *De Processibus,* pp. 581-582.

[46] Blat, *Commentarium Textus Codicis Iuris Canonici,* Lib. IV *De Processibus,* 526.

[47] Roberti, *De Processibus,* I, 67; Kay, *Competence in Matrimonial Procedure,* 128.

mentation for their view; their arguments have been duly considered throughout the whole of this chapter.[48]

If numbers alone could indicate the proper answer, the administrative view would be easily established; unfortunately, however, most of these authors merely state their belief, without adding substantiating reasons. From Many (1919)[49] to Linneborn (1933)[50] there has been a tradition favoring the administrative nature and supported by such authors as Vlaming,[51] Chelodi,[52] Cerato,[53] Koeninger,[54] Farrugia,[55] Lanier,[56] Prümmer,[57] Payen,[58] Gasparri,[59] De Smet,[60] Cappello,[61] Wernz-Vidal.[62] As will

[48] Triebs, "De interpretatione canonum 1990-1992," *Periodica,* XX (1931), 93*-107* and "Das summarische Verfahren in kanonischen Eheprozess auf Grund der canones 1990-1992 C. J. C."—*Theol. Quartal.,* CXIII (1931), 207-223. Kay, *Competence in Matrimonial Procedure,* 109-142.

[49] "l'affaire se traite *extraiudicialiter,* en dehors de tout jugement." Note de Msgr. Many, 31 Dec. 1919—*Le Mariage Chretien,* Fourneret, 457-458.

[50] Linneborn, *Grundriss des Eherechts,* 471, footnote 2.

[51] "Praesenti vero canone remittuntur quaelibet solemnitates hucusque (in Codice) recensitae, hinc etiam illae quae spectant ad ordinem iudicialem universim . . . Igitur conceditur ut . . . nonnisi administrative, uti aiunt, procedatur."—Vlaming, *Praelectiones Iuris Matrimonii,* II, 384.

[52] "Declaratio administrativa . . . ius concedit ut procedatur simplici modo administrativo."—Chelodi, *Ius Matrimoniale,* n. 195.

[53] ". . . procedere licet simplici modo, ut dicitur, *administrativo."*—Cerato, *Matrimonium,* 261.

[54] ". . . in these cases there is only necessary a summary or more accurately, a declaratory process . . ."—Koeniger-Giese, *Grundzüge des katholischen Kirchenrechts,* 155.

[55] Farrugia, *De Matrimonio et Causis Matrimonialibus,* 533.

[56] "C'est une procédure administrative . . .;" "Le juge de seconde instance décidera . . . toujours par consequent *modo administrativo . . ."* —Lanier, *Procédure Matrimoniale,* 2 and 4.

[57] ". . . quando autem obstat matrimonio unam ex septem impedimentis . . ., non est necessarius processus iudicialis."—Prümmer, *Manuale Iuris Canonici,* 629.

[58] ". . . integrum est Ordinario loci procedere *modo mere administrativo,* seu declarare sine *ullo* processu iudiciali, matrimonii nullitatem."—Payen, *De Matrimonio,* II, 530.

[59] "Codex . . . decernit . . . Ordinarium, praetermissis cuiusque generis solemnitatibus, seu quovis processu iudiciali, matrimonii nullitatem decla-

be seen from the quotations from their works, these authors consider the title—*De casibus exceptis a regulis hucusque traditis* and the text—*praetermissis solemnitatibus hucusque recensitis,* as liberating from all judicial forms. Cappello and Many proffer other arguments which have been incorporated in the earlier parts of this chapter, Cocchi[63] and Vermeesch-Creusen[64] merely restate the arguments for both views, judicial and administrative, without adopting either; however, an answer in the *Periodica,* presumably written by Vermeesch, admits the administrative view.[65] It is merely from indications here and there in these authors that the present chapter has been partly constructed, for no arguments have been developed to any length by these writers.

2. *Replies to several difficulties.*

On October 19, 1919, the Pontifical Commission explained that no judicial process nor the intervention of the *Defensor vinculi* were required, when a declaration of nullity was to be rendered for marriages in which the proper ecclesiastical form had been entirely neglected.[66] Authors, favoring the judicial

---

rare posse . . ."—Gasparri, *De Matrimonio,* II, 306.

[60] ". . . nullitas potest . . . ab Ordinario declarari, quin praecedere debeat juridicus processus."—De Smet in *ETL,* I (1924), 578.

[61] His arguments have appeared earlier in this chapter. Cf. Cappello, *De Sacramentis,* III, 1011-1021, and "De Casibus Exceptis ad normam canonum 1990-1992," *Jus Pontificium,* XII (1932), 106-113.

[62] ". . . conceditur ut possit procedi . . . *modo administrativo* qui a solemnitatibus rigiosi processus iudicialis est absolutus."—Wernz-Vidal, *Jus Canonicum,* V, 842.

[63] Cocchi, *De Processibus,* 487-488.

[64] Vermeersch-Creusen, *Epitome Iuris Canonici,* III, 135.

[65] "Canon 1990 permittit ut in locum processus stricte iudicialis, forma potius administrativa assumatur declarandi . . ."—*Periodica,* XIII (1924), (211).

[66] "Utrum Ordinarium praetermissis iuris solemnitatibus in Constitutione Apostolica *Dei Miseratione* requisitis, matrimonium possit declarare nullum, cum interventu tamen defensoris vinculi matrimonialis, quin opus sit secunda instantia, hisce in casibus, nempe: . . . Resp. Casus supranumer-

view of canons 1990-1992, argue that this response substantiates their view, because they consider the *dubium* to have been submitted in connection with canon 1990 and therefore "in a contrary sense . . . the process in canon 1990 must be judicial by nature."[67] This argument does not seem valid for the following reasons. Without doubt, the absence of the old impediment of clandestinity from the list of 1990 cases was the occasion for this *dubium*: if that canon, which represented the older summary process, omitted cases of non-observance of the due form, how were such cases to be handled? Here, it is contended by the present author, any connection with canon 1990 ceased: the *dubium* is not based on this canon, but on the older and clearly judicial process. To establish this contention, study of the language of the *dubium* is necessary. Since canon 1990 excluded these cases, it was necessary to learn just how they were to be handled. In the formation of the *dubium*, the possibility of reviewing such cases under canon 1990 evidently was not contemplated, for otherwise the *dubium* could easily have been worded to ask whether canon 1990 would be extended to include clandestinity or not. The solution hit upon was to determine whether the older law of the Holy Office (June 5, 1889), permitting a special procedure for clandestine marriages, could still be used. Those who proposed the *dubium* harkened back to this former order, as is clear from their use of the older terminology, viz., *praetermissis iuris solemnitatibus in constitutione Dei miseratione requisitis* or practically a quotation from the 1889 decree of the Holy Office. This should not be taken as an equivalent way of referring to canon 1990, for the language is not that of canon 1990.

---

ati nullum iudicialem processum requirunt aut interventum Defensoris vinculi, sed resolvendi sunt ab Ordinario ipso, vel a parocho, consulto Ordinario, in praevia investigatione ad matrimanii celebrationem, de qua in can. 1019 et seqq. Pont. Comm. Interp. Cod., 16 Oct., 1919, ad 17—*AAS*, XI (1919), 479.

[67] Kay, *op. cit.*, 137; Noval, *op. cit.*, n. 873; Triebs, "Actio ex cc. 1990-1992 Iudicialis Probatur," *Periodica*, XX (1931), 104.*

It is indisputable that this special process of old, was judicial, especially in view of the several declarations of the Holy See.[68] In answering this *dubium*—"could clandestine marriages be tried as of old?"—the Pontifical Commission permitted a new type of treatment, i. e., a simple, administrative investigation and denied that the former discipline, represented in the *dubium,* any longer governed such cases (*casus . . . nullum iudicialem processum requirunt . . .*). In brief, the *dubium* was not based on canon 1990 and accordingly any "contrary" argument making this canon judicial is invalid: the *nullum iudicialem processum* must refer to the older procedure of 1889, which included clandestinity among its cases.

Probably the strongest argument in favor of the judicial character of canons 1990-1992, is the inference drawn from a reply of the *Praeses* of the Pontifical Commission for the Authentic Interpretation of the Code, December 19, 1923. This reply was sent to the *Officialis* of the Curia of Paris, whose competence to decide the 1990-cases had been challenged by the *Defensor;* the *Officialis* had resigned his office as Vicar-General and so was restricted to the hearing of judicial matters.[69] Here are reproduced the sections of the query and of the reply that deals directly with the problem.

1. Quum can. 1990 Ordinario potestatem faciat declarandi de plano nullitatem in hisce casibus, an Officialis servet facultatem diiudicandi, servato iuris ordine, huiusmodi casus qui illi delati fuerint?

Et quatenus affirmative:

2. An lata ab Officiali sententia nullitatis, teneatur Defensor vinculi ad interponendam appellationem ex officio, etsi pateat nullitatem matrimonii esse evidentem?

---

[68] S. C. S. Off. *Albanen. in America,* 10 Jun. 1896—*Fontes,* n. 1180.
S. C. Concilii, 16 Jun. 1894.—*ASS,* XXVII (1894-1895), 153.
S. C. S. Off., 27 Mart. 1901—*Fontes,* n. 1251.

[69] ". . . étant Official de la Curie de Paris, mais ayant cessé à cette épouye d'étre Vicàire Général pour me consacrer exclusivement aux causes judiciares, le droit m' a été contesté dijuger sommairement d'aprés le Canon 1990 les causes de nullité de mariage évidente."—Kay, *op. cit.,* 139.

3. An saltem, introducta causa coram Tribunali, possit aut etiam debeat Officialis, statim ac adverterit nullitatem esse evidentem, acta causae, in quocumque statu inveniantur, tradere Ordinario qui evidentem nullitatem declaret absque solemnitatibus?

Et quatenus affirmative:

4. An Defensor vinculi, eo quod causa iudicialiter incepta fuerit, possit aut debeat huiusmodi traditioni se opponere, et deinde, lata ab Ordinario sententia appellationem ex officio necessario interponere?

These questions were rearranged in Rome and answered as follows:

Cum dubia circa causas matrimoniales quae proposuisti ad hanc Commissionem, quadam aequivocatione laborant, visum est ea posse reformari, prout sequitur:

1°—Utrum in casibus de quibus in Canone 1990, necesse sit ut loci Ordinarius per se evidentem matrimonii nullitatem declaret an id possit ipsemet Officialis?

2°—Utrum in iisdem casibus Ordinarius possit procedere ad ordinariam tramitem iuris?

4°—An per iudicem secundae instantiae, de quo Can. 1991, intelligi debeat Ordinarius Dioecesis ad appellationem designatae aut Officialis, aut Tribunal Collegiale huius Dioecesis?

Porro hisce dubiis, infrascriptus Emus Commissionis Praeses respondit:

Ad 1 am. Negative ad partem Iam; affirmative ad secundam salvo praescripto Canonis 1573 §2.

Ad 2 am. Negative et serventur Can. 1990-1991.

Ad 4 am. Est Metropolita vel loci Ordinarius ad appellationem designatus ad normam Can. 1594 § 1-§ 2 firma hoc quoque in casu responsione ad Iam.

Quae dum Tibi, Reverendissime Domine, significo, cuncta bona a Deo deprecor.

Sign. Petrus Card. Gasparri, Praeses,
A Card. Sincero, Pro Secretarius.[70]

---

[70] Kay, *Competence in Matrimonial Procedure*, 139-141.

From the queries proposed, it is not entirely clear whether an administrative or judicial notion was presupposed; the prominent point seems to be whether the word *Ordinarius* of canon 1990 had effectively reserved those evident cases to the personal judgment of the Bishop, or whether the *Officialis* could still judge them using the formal marriage trial (cf. *servato iuris ordine*: *ex officio appellationem* of the *Defensor*: *possit aut etiam debeat . . . acta . . . tradere Ordinario*). It is just this particular which is emphasized in the first of the recast questions: "*Utrum . . . necesse sit ut Ordinarius per se . . . declaret an id possit ipsemet Officialis?*" The replies to this and to the fourth questions settle directly that the Code has not reserved the 1990-cases to the personal judgment of the Bishop; the *Officialis* may handle these cases. From this response, it has been argued that the power exercised for these evident cases must be judicial, for otherwise, the *Officialis* would not be competent to act.[71]

It must be confessed that this conclusion seems justified, especially in view of the invoking of canon 1573 § 2 which identifies the *Officialis* as the judge of the diocesan tribunal with the Bishop. Accordingly, any Bishop who assumes that his *Officialis* is competent by his very appointment as judge to handle the cases of canon 1990 has the authority of this rescript to support him.

It is believed, however, that this reply does not settle the dispute regarding the character of the power exercised in canon 1990 and to offset the impression favoring the judicial character, the following observation may be in order. This reply was rendered by the *Praeses* alone and of course, has equal force to a decision of the Commission acting as a body;[72] yet it is easier to catch the meaning behind an individual mind than that of a corporate mind and so a reference to Cardinal Gasparri's writings is useful. Here, nine years after his reply to the Curia of Paris, the Cardinal implies that the process of canons 1990-1992

---

[71] Kay, *Competence in Matrimonial Procedure,* 141-142.

[72] Cicognani, *Canon Law,* 435.

is administrative;[73] although he does not write as *Praeses,* his opinion in this treatise may not be entirely divorced from his decision as *Praeses.* On the supposition that the reply of 1923 indicates the judicial character of canons 1990-1992, one must admit a change in the Cardinal's opinion. On the strength of this change, it might reasonably be expected that, if such a question were submitted at present, the Commission would safeguard the administrative character of the process; a change in the responses of the Commission is not altogether impossible.[74]

[73] ". . . Codex . . . decernit . . . Ordinarium, praetermissis cuiusque generis solemnitatibus, seu *quovis processu iudiciali,* matrimonii nullitatem declarare posse . . ." Gasparri, *De Matrimonio* (ed nova), II, p. 306.

[74] Some authors would see such a change in the responses regarding Canon 1098: Respon. Pont. Commiss., 10 Martii 1928, *AAS,* XX (1928), 120 and 25 Julii 1931, *AAS,* XXIII (1931), 388.

It is interesting to note that Lanier, *Vice-Official* of the Curia of *Paris* when he wrote in 1927, interprets the word *Ordinarius* as not including the *Officialis* (à l'Ordinaire, et non à l'Officiale *ut sic*); also note that Mons. Sabatier, *Vicar General and Official of the Paris* Curia, commends the author in a preface, recalling "J'ai dit: manuel pratique. Il sera le fruit *de votre expérience* personelle et de l'expérience de tous ceux qui ont passé *dans cette Officialité de Paris.*"—Lanier, *Guide Pratique de la Procédure Matrimoniale,* pp. vii-ix; 2 and 4.

CHAPTER IV

THE PROCEDURE OF CANONS 1990-1992

In view of the general tone of the Title to Chapter VII (*De casibus exceptis a regulis hucusque traditis*) and of the text (*praetermissis solemnitatibus hucusque recensitis*), there has been some uncertainty regarding the proper method of procedure under canons 1990-1992. This has been particularly the difficulty of those who maintain that these canons represent a judicial process: these authors vary in noting how much of the regular matrimonial trial must be retained lest the process be invalid, e. g., whether a notary *must* be present, whether a priest, if he is to gather evidence, *must* be delegated, whether the decision of the case *must* be drawn up in a certain form, whether the rules of competence *must* be followed, etc. In the view of the author and of others who believe that the process of canons 1900-1992 is administrative, these difficulties vanish; no longer is there required the observance of *any* of the judicial prescriptions, save those mentioned in canon 1990 (*citatis partibus and cum interventu defensoris vinculi*) which are to be observed only that the process be properly conducted. The neglect of these two would not render the proceedings null as in administrative matters the Ordinary is not held to any special rules under pain of nullity; he is to administer his diocese freely and often he must act speedily when the observance of the rules necessary for valid acts would contravene the purpose of this expeditious act (the regulations for the liceity of course would give way because of the necessity of the case). Accordingly great freedom must be admitted in the mode of conducting the process of canons 1990-1992 and what is hereafter set down is merely suggestive of the better methods which in some instances are obligatory for the liceity of the process. There shall be four divisions in this treatment, viz.:

ARTICLE I. THE PERSONS INVOLVED IN THESE CANONS

1. *Competent Ordinary* (. . . *poterit Ordinarius . . . matrimonii declarare nullitatem.*)

All those of Canon 198 § 1 are "competent" to act in this special marriage process, viz.: the residential Bishop, Abbots and Prelates *nullius,* Vicars General, Administrators, Vicars and Prefects Apostolic (and their Vicars Delegate, Pro-Vicars and Pro-prefects). Of those just mentioned, a special word should be said regarding the Vivar General (and his missionary counterpart, the Vicar Delegate). Since the process is believed to be administrative, the Vicar General may conduct the process by virtue of his office as assistant administrator to the Bishop; (Canon 366 § 1; 368 § 1) he may act whenever the *Ordinarius* is mentioned, unless he is expressly excluded and in respect to canon 1990, he has not been excluded because the process is not judicial (Canon 1573 § 1) and because the Bishop has not reserved these cases to himself. No contradiction can be seen in so admitting the Vicar General, for on the one hand he should be the ablest man in the diocese next to the Bishop and on the other hand, these cases are of evident nullity not requiring a specialist's knowledge of judicial processes. Nevertheless it would be better if the *Officialis* were enabled to handle canon 1990 cases both because the Vicar General is generally burdened with the affairs of the diocese and because the handling of nullity-proceedings in marriage causes is the very work of the *Officialis*. In the decree of his appointment as *Officialis* should be given special delegation to act under canon 1990 (not as a judicial personage, but as sharing in the administration of the diocese).[1]

For ordinary marriage trials, the rules of competence contained in canon 1964 are so obligatory that their neglect renders the trial invalid (e. g., the judge is relatively incompetent, canon 1559 § 2, but he may declare himself competent, canon 1616 § 2 or may "heal" the sentence, invalid because of his relative incompetence, canon 1892, 1°); in the administrative action of canon 1990 there is no obligation, as in canon 1609 § 1, to determine such competence. The Ordinary may handle any matrimonial case that falls under canon 1990 even though none of the conditions of canon 1964 would be fulfilled (e. g., the defendant may not be a subject of the Ordinary) because these rules of canon 1964 apply only to a judicial matter. Still the exercise of canon 1990 is not entirely unregulated so that an Ordinary could handle any petition which is presented to him without further investigation; administrative acts are to be regulated by canon 201 § 1 and § 3 which permit direct action (even administratively) only over subjects[2] whether these presented the

[1] If the *Officialis* acts without this special authorization, the proceedings will not be invalid as "competence" will be supplied as long as the matter of the nature of the process is disputed. Favoring the *Officialis* as competent because he has been delegated as judge are, Noval, *De Iudiciis*, p. 581; Triebs, "Actio ex cc. 1990-1992 Iudicialis Probatur", *Periodica*, XX (1931), 93*-107*; Kay, *Competence in Matrimonial Procedure*, p. 152. Until this dispute is settled, the Officialis will also be competent; cf. the response to the Curia of Paris, *supra*, pp. 73-76.

[2] Maroto, *Institutiones*, I, n. 727; Ojetti, *Commentarium*, IV, p. 183.

petition or were the defendants. Apparently this canon is broad enough to permit an Ordinary to handle marriage-cases of non-subjects, administratively, as long as an interested third party is his subject, in as much as the canon acknowledges an indirect jurisdiction;[3] an example of this would be: "*C*, a subject, wishes to marry *B*, a non-subject, whose previous marriage to *A*, a non-subject, is to be investigated."

It is quite possible, however, that the Holy See may enjoin the observance of canon 1964 for the special process of canon 1990, yet this would not necessarily prove the judicial nature of canons 1990-1992, but merely would indicate a practical rule. Until such an instruction, canon 1964 should not be imposed in this administrative proceedings and there will be little difficulty in the matter of shifting of responsibilities from diocese to diocese when it is remembered that an Ordinary is "competent" under canon 1990 only when either the petitioner or defendant is his subject, in view of canon 201 §1.

Canon 1990, in stating that *Ordinarius poterit declarare,* evidently is granting a favor and due to the great saving of time it is hardly necessary to remark that he ought to use this favor without scruple, as often as possible; despite the word *poterit,* it seems clear that there is an obligation to use this process for the sake of the parties' spiritual welfare and to save them the otherwise useless expense of the regular procedure, so much so that if a case has been commenced in the regular trial and develops as one of canon 1990 cases it should be settled at once by canon 1990.[4]

2. *Competent Petitioner*

In as much as canon 1990 is not a judicial process, the one who introduces the case may not be called an *actor;* hereafter, he or she shall be referred to as the petitioner.

---

[3] Maroto, *op. cit.,* I, n. 727; *Ojetti, op. cit.,* IV, p. 183.

[4] Kay, *Competence,* 152; Cappello adopts contrary view in *De Matrimonio,* (1933), III, p. 1016.

In the regular matrimonial trial non-Catholics may not act as *actores* unless special permission has been previously obtained from the Holy See.[5] Furthermore, when both parties to the marriage are non-Catholics it would seem that the non-Catholic having obtained such a permission must introduce his cause before that Bishop who is the Ordinary of the Catholic party desirous of the marriage, a rule already accepted before June 23, 1903, and repeated on April 8, 1925.[6] In the canon 1990 process, it is submitted that no permission need be sought from the Holy See for non-Catholics to act as petitioners; the prohibition of January 27, 1928 does not include the cases of canons 1990-1992 as is clear from the response of the Holy Office to a *dubium* cast in general terms (April 14, 1931) and from the arguments based on another rescript to the Bishop of Harrisburg.[7]

When a non-Catholic requests a judgment of the validity of his former marriage under canon 1990 so as to be free to marry a Catholic or to have his second marriage with a Catholic convalidated, the Ordinary may handle the petition without authorization from the Holy See or without recourse to the theory of *causa connexa.* As mentioned before it does not seem necessary that the non-Catholic present his petition before the Ordinary of the Catholic party interested in the second marriage, for in the reply to the *dubium* of April 14, 1931, no mention is made of this rule but the Bishop is simply mentioned as ''competent'' to handle any petition of a non-Catholic that occurs (. . . *casus*

---

[5] Resp. S. C. S. Off., 27 Jan. 1928-*AAS,* XX (1928), 75.

[6] "Quando vero agitur de matrimonio mixto contrahendo cum haeretico separato per divortii sententiam tribunalis civilis ab heretica, erit Episcopus domicilii partis catholicae, ad quem spectat iudicare an contrahentes gaudeant statua libertate."- Resp. Cong. S. R. et U. Inquisitionis, 23 Junii 1903—Fontes, n. 1266. cf. Resp. eiusdem Congreg. ad Archiepis. Friburgen., 8 Aprilis 1925—*AfkK,* CVII (1927), 569-574 and above, Chap. III.

[7] Resp. S. C. S. Off., 14 April, 1931, private (cf. *supra,* pp. 62-67). Resp. S. C. S. Off. ad Epis. Harrisb., 20 Aprilis 1931—*AER,* LXXXVI (1932), 68-73.

quosdam apud istam Revmam Curiam Episcopalem examinandos occurrere . . .).

3. *Defensor's role* [8]

From the historical section of this study, it is evident that the Holy See has always insisted on the intervention of the *Defensor Vinculi* whether the simplified process was authorized as an administrative or as a judicial matter; this insistence, no doubt, was due to the desire to safeguard the sacredness of marriages. The Code has likewise retained the *Defensor,* despite the liberation from every other judicial form (except the citation of the parties); since the Code has specified the presence of the *Defensor* there does not seem to be any justification for the practice of neglecting him. In accordance with the remarks above, failure to use the *Defensor* would not render the "sentence" invalid; nevertheless there is an obligation to invoke his aid for the proper (licit) conducting of the process.[9] To accept the obligation of having the *Defensor* act in each case is not to maintain that all the formalities attendant on the *Defensor* in the regular trial must be observed in canon 1990. The canon requires the intervention of the *Defensor* which seems to be amply fulfilled if all the documents and proofs are presented, as a completed case, to the *Defensor* for his study and if he has an opportunity of expressing his opinion to the Ordinary regarding the certainty of the proof.[10] In as much as the formalities of the regular trial are to be overlooked, the office of the *Defensor* will be correspondingly simplified; thus he need not be cited nor are there any sessions which he must attend nor will he be required to make the summing up (*discussio causae*); of course as a member of the diocesan Curia he should take the oath of office for each case, if he has not already done so, *semel pro*

---

[8] Cf. Dolan, *The Defensor Vinculi,* Washington D. C., 1934, pp. 126-129.

[9] Cappello, *De Matrimonio,* III, n. 891, 3; Payen, *De Matrimonio,* II, n. 2723, 2, 2o.

[10] Vlaming, *Praelectiones Iuris Matrimonii,* II, n. 803.

semper.[11] The duty of the *Defensor* is well expressed in these words; ". . . he must ascertain that the document is truly genuine and that it is properly valuated. He should also make certain that the document really applies to the case. . . . he of course, when necessary, may attack the documents as forgeries, or attack the signatures, or strive to forestall any other attempt to perpetrate fraud . . ."[12] The discussion, if any, is informal with no obligation, e. g., of submitting questions signed and sealed (Canon 1968) nor of presenting additional questions through the judge (Canon 1773 § 1-§ 2); if the *Defensor* should wish to interrogate the parties or witnesses, e. g., to prove the identity of the parties, he may do so informally and directly. Satisfied that the impediment existed at the time of the marriage and that the marriage was not in any way convalidated, the *Defensor* returns the proofs to the Ordinary who may then render his decision. The particular duties of the *Defensor* with regard to each of the impediments will be remarked in a later section dealing with these impediments.

At times the *Defensor* may not be satisfied with the documents or the proofs and should so advise the Ordinary; apparently the Ordinary may disregard his opinion and declare the nullity of the marriage. If the Ordinary so acts, the *Defensor* must "appeal" and arrange for the transmission of all the *acta* to the judge of the second instance; incidentally, this need of an "appeal" will rarely occur unless the *Defensor* is rather scrupulous, as the proofs for canon 1990 cases will generally be clear.

According to canon 1992, the *Defensor* of the diocese to which the case has been transferred reviews the case with his Ordinary even as had the *Defensor* in the first instance: there are no added requirements for this rehearing; in fact, even the citation of the parties may be omitted as shall be argued in the following number.

---

[11] Canon 364 § 2, 1°; even though he would not be obliged to the oath for canon 1990, from the prescription of canon 1621 § 1 which regulates a judicial matter. Cf. "Quaesita Varia" in *Periodica*, XIII (1924), 212.

[12] Dolan, *The Defensor Vinculi*, 78.

4. *Citation of the Parties*

Even though canon 1990 would seem to have clearly prescribed the citation of the parties, yet the Pontifical Commission was asked whether this citation must be made before the declaration of nullity; naturally, the answer merely confirmed the prescription of the canon.[13] Just why the question was asked is not clear, although one of the following two reasons may have been the motive. It had been said that this *citatio* was not required whenever the rights of the defendant were safeguarded or whenever the case was sufficiently proved by the evidence introduced by the petitioner;[14] the Pontifical Commission may have responded in order to emphasize that even in such a case, the parties should be cited so that both might know of the declaration of the nullity. Perhaps the suggestion of Creusen would explain the response: as the words *citatis partibus* had been inserted between *Ordinarius* and *declarare,* it might have seemed that the parties were to be cited only when the decree of nullity was about to be read. As such a special citation (though provided for in canons 1724 and 1877) falls far short of the proper purpose of a citation, scil., the safeguarding of the rights of the parties and the obtaining of certitude, the Commission may have wished to indicate an earlier citation, before the Ordinary has come to formulate and express his declaration of nullity (*ante declarationem*).[15]

There can be no doubt but that the parties must be cited, and it is generally believed that this citation is not to be made merely that the parties hear the declaration (as in canon 1877)

---

[13] "Utrum *citatio partium* de qua in can. 1990, facienda sit ante declarationem nullitatis matrimonii. Resp. Affirmative"—Pont. Commis. 16 Jun. 1931—*AAS,* XXIII (1931), 354; Roberti, "De Nullitatis Matrimonii Declaratione," *Appollinaris,* IV (1931), 380.

[14] Vlaming, *Praelectiones Iuris Matrimonii,* II, p. 385, footnote 1.

[15] Creusen, "Les Déclarations de Nullité de Mariage, 16 Jul. 1931," *NRT,* LVIII (1931), 827; Cappello, *De Matrimonio,* III, n. 891, 3; Ayrinhac-Lydon, *Marriage Legislation,* p. 364; " A Recent Decision", *IER,* LXVII (1932), 536.

but rather that both may know of the action and offer possible objections or help in clarifying particulars of the documents (e. g., checking signatures).[16] Ordinarily under canon 1990 the defendant would not have to be cited for clarifying of the case, as these impediments will be evident nor for the safeguarding of his other rights as a previous divorce will generally have occurred and will be ample evidence of his or her attitude; nevertheless the citation must be made or at least attempted, in accord with the canon and the response of the Pontifical Commission.

It would seem that this citation may be made in any convenient mode, without the obligation of observing the details of canon 1715 under penalty of rendering the declaration null;[17] this seems to follow from the fact that these rules are for trials (whilst canon 1990 is not a *trial*) and that all solemnities of the regular trial are expressly dispensed with in canon 1990 (*praetermissis solemnitatibus hucusque recensitis*).[18]

Because it is foreseen that a citation will be useless or that the party may not be reached (e. g., since his abode is unknown), it is not therefore permissible to omit the act completely; at least, an *effort* should be made to acquaint the party of the action being taken on his or her marriage. Refusal to appear upon learning of the process from the citation suffices for the fulfillment of the obligation[19] as does the unsuccessful effort to locate the party; in as much as this citation is required for the lawful, not valid, carrying out of the process, such an effort should be sufficient[20] without the *solemnity* of *citatio per edictum* of canon 1720.[21]

---

16 Triebs, "Actio ex cc. 1990-1992 iudicialis probatur," *Periodica,* XX (1931), 100; and Vermeesch, "Adnotationes, . . . De nullitate matrimonii declaranda," *Periodica,* XXI (1932), 40.

17 Canon 1723.

18 Vlaming, *Praelectiones,* II, p. 385; *e contra:* Kay, *Competence in Matrimonial Procedure,* 152; "The Necessity for a Citation, etc." *IER,* XXVII (1926), 529.

19 Canon 1718.

20 Nau, *Marriage Laws of the Code,* 226.

21 Payen, *De Matrimonio,* III, n. 2723, 1.

The citation does not seem to be required if the case is carried to the second hearing (Canons 1991-1992); it might appear that the citation was to be made in view of these words of canon 1992 "... *decernit eodem modo de quo in can.* 1990" and this has been maintained by some authors.[22] That the citation may be omitted seems far more likely: because the word *solo* has been added to *interventu Defensoris,* thereby excluding something of canon 1990 and the only act that could be excluded evidently is the citation of the parties; because as a matter of fact the words *citatis partibus* have been omitted; because there would not have been any reason to add *interventu Defensoris* if the words *eodem modo de quo in can.* 1990 were to be referred to the *Defensor* and *citatio* rather than to the *praetermissis solemnitatibus;* because the Pontifical Commission referred in its response only to the citation of canon 1990 (merely confirmatory); because canon 1992 is revisional, i. e., "is the doubt of the *Defensor* on this case as transmitted reasonable or not," so that there is no need of further investigation.[23] *In praxi,* there will rarely occur such a second hearing in canon 1990 cases which are either evident or must be handed directly to the regular procedure.

ARTICLE II. THE IMPEDIMENTS THEMSELVES

Before the impediments are treated individually, it is well to set down some general remarks that apply in a varying degree to all the impediments, viz., the nature of the proofs, documentary and oral, the lack of a dispensation and the definitive (*taxative*) listing of the impediments.

1. *The Proofs*
(*Cum ex certo et authentico documento ...*)

From the wording of the canon, it would seem that the only admissible proofs are documents, so much so that this procedure

[22] Vermeesch-Creusen, *Epitome,* III, n. 297; Noval, *De Processibus* n. 875.

[23] Blat, *De Processibus,* IV, n. 553; Cappello, *De Matrimonio,* III, n. 891.

has been called "the Documental Process;"[24] this view seems to be confirmed because the legislator has omitted in Canon 1990 the words, . . . *vel in huius defectu ex certis argumentis* . . ., which permitted other means of proof before the Code.[25] Kay modifies this strict view by remarking that ". . . testimony of persons does not seem contrary to the regulations of the Code as long as this type of proof is secondary and does not *supply in the points where documents can and should be had"*;[26] from the tenor of his following sentences, it seems that he would not admit testimony when *positive* facts are to be proved, but documents are lacking. It is just here that a step forward should be taken, viz., testimony and valid presumptions should be admitted not merely to prove negative facts but even to supply for the lack of documents which ordinarily would be at hand for positive facts (e. g., for a record of a baptism).

To support this further step, the following arguments may be advanced. If the words of the canon, *ex certo et authentico documento,* were meant to be interpreted strictly to the exclusion of any proof but documentary, then the canon would be self-contradictory in this respect, that disparity of cult is included but could never be established (because no document will be available establishing the non-baptism of the marriage-partner). Whilst this concerns but a negative fact and could not be applied with equal force to positive facts, it at least reveals that the word *documento* must not be considered as prohibiting all other types of proof. Again, the document must be certain (*certo*) in its reference to the impediment and to the person involved; testimony is thereby apparently demanded by the very canon because it is practically only through testimony that *this* petitioner can be identified as the same person mentioned in the document (i. e., that no substitution of persons has occurred). To these two leading arguments may be added the weight of most authorities: as far as could be discovered, no

---

24 Roberti, *De Processibus,* I, p. 67.

25 S. C. S. Off., 5 Jun. 1889—*Fontes* n. 1118.

26 Kay, *Competence in Matrimonial Procedure,* 146 (italics mine).

author explicitly denies that other proof may be utilized; Noval merely comments on the text as do Blat and Wernz-Vidal.[27] From the response of the Pontifical Commission [28] some authors would argue backwards in this wise: if the certitude of no dispensation, obtained by proofs other than documentary, is admitted as of equal weight to the certitude regarding the existence of the impediment, then in turn it should be permissible to obtain this latter certitude by testimony and valid presumptions.[29] Other authors already before this response of the Pontifical Commission had admitted non-documentary proofs, recalling the rule in use before the Code.[30] In view of these arguments, it is permissible to utilize witnesses and valid presumptions whenever documents are lacking; undoubtedly the ordinary course should be to secure documents and only in their defect should other proofs be substituted. The application of this view will be remarked in the subsequent treatment of each impediment.

With regard to witnesses, the following remarks of Nau [31] are quite in place: "Not infrequently non-Catholics refuse to appear before a priest, but will go to a civil notary public. The Ordinary can delegate a given notary public. Non-Catholics sometimes will appear only before a notary of their own choosing. In such cases care must be taken that there is no substitution of parties . . . and that an oath is really administered. It

---

[27] Noval, *De Processibus*, n. 873; Blat, *De Processibus*, n. 551; Wernz-Vidal, *Jus Matrimoniale*, p. 842.

[28] "Utrum par certitudo de qua in canone 1990, haberi possit tantum ex certo et authentico documento;—an etiam ex alio legitimo modo. Resp. Negative ad primam partem; affirmative ad secundam". Resp. Pont. Commis. 16 Jul. 1931—*AAS*, XXIII (1931), 353.

[29] Gasparri, *De Matrimonio*, (ed. nova), II, p. 306; Mussener, *Das Katholische Eherecht*, p. 173; Nau, *Marriage Laws of the Code*, pp. 229-230; Vermeesch, "Adnotationes, . . . De nullitate matrimonii declaranda," *Periodica*, XXI (1932), 40; Cappello, *De Matrimonio*, III, n. 891, 6°.

[30] Vermeesch-Creusen, *Epitome*, III, n. 296; Payen, *De Matrimonio*, III, n. 2722, 2, 2°; "De causis Matrimonialibus in missionibus exteris," *Periodica*, XIII (1924), (210)-(212).

[31] *Marriage Laws of the Code*, pp. 229-230.

is of the utmost importance that a proper questionnaire be submitted. . . . Testimony before an authorized priest has much more value than before a civil notary.[32] However, in some cases it might be well to have the sanction of civil law to lend fear of prosecution before the civil law in case of perjury."

It seems fitting that an estimate of the witness' character and veracity should be obtained either from the person who received the deposition or from the witness' pastor if possible or from two reliable persons acquainted with the witness. Of course, this means difficulties but as can readily be seen in such matters of conscience care must be exercised.

The Documents[33]

A document is best defined as any writing from which a fact may be proved;[34] it hardly seems necessary that the writing have been made for the future purpose of establishing some fact, for then private writings could never be admitted as proofs (e. g., letters written *tempore non suspecto*).[35]

Some take the word *authentico* as equivalent to "genuine" or to "true"[36] so that private documents could be admitted without further trouble once they were proven genuine (i. e., actually written by the one whose signature appears). It seems rather that the word *authentico* should be accepted with most cononists, as referring to a document that produces full (public) faith or proof:[37] this seems the more proper sense of the word

32 In as much as the process is non-judicial, authorization or delegation of a priest as *auditor* is not required, and there seems to be no reason why such an undelegated priest may not proffer the oath *de veritate dicendi vel dictorum* (as the process is non-judicial).

33 Kay treats this subject fully in *Competence in Matrimonial Procedure*, 142-147.

34 Noval, *De Processibus*, n. 551.

35 Vermeesch-Creusen, *Epitome*, III, n. 198.

36 Lydon, *Marriage Legislation*, p. 363; Blat, *De Processibus*, n. 551.

37 Noval, *op. cit.*, p. 366, 2; Vermeesch-Creusen, *Epitome*, III, n. 296, 2; Cappello, *De Matrimonio*, III, n. 891, 3; Vlaming, *Praelectiones*, II, n. 803; Payen, *De Matrimonio*, III, n. 2722, 1, b.

when the usage of the Code itself is considered; for canons 1813 § 1, 4° and 1819 speak of *authentic* copies of public documents as equivalent to the documents themselves and of equal proving value; and in a separate canon (1814), the Code remarks that such public documents (or their authentic equivalents) are to be presumed *genuine,* thus distinguishing between *authentic* and *genuine.* Generally, such authentic documents will be public ones, viz., witnessed or signed by a competent public personage (i. e., duly executed)and these may be either ecclesiastical or civil according to the ecclesiastical or civil character of the public witness. Selected from the outline in canon 1813, examples of public church documents having place in canon 1990 are the dispensations granted by various Congregations (e. g., the Congregation for Religious and the Congregation of the Sacraments), dispensations from impediments granted by the Ordinary and all those records of sacraments received or of deaths; such records produce the full proof accorded them by law whether they are the originals or transcripts properly signed by a public church person. Public civil records of use in canon 1990 are health records (birth and death records), registers of marriage licenses, of marriages and of divorces or affidavits sworn to before a public notary; these also may be presented either in the original (rarely) or in properly attested copies (canon 1819).

As a rule private documents (those written by private persons or by public officials without the requisite formalities) are not to be admitted in canon 1990 in as much as they are not authentic (though genuine and possibly true) and so *per se* do not produce full proof (canons 1816-1817). To be admitted, such private documents should be raised to the equivalent of public documents by having the contents of the private writing sworn to as true before a notary, civil or ecclesiastical.[38] Short of such official approbation, what part may private documents play in canon 1990? From canon 1817, it is clear that such documents may prove *against* their author, once they have been acknowl-

[38] Noval, *De Processibus,* n. 551.

edged as genuine; e. g., a petition for a declaration of nullity under canon 1990 due to disparity of cult may be rejected because the Ordinary is acquainted with a letter of the petitioner describing, e. g., what fun was had when a number of young folk submitted to a baptismal rite (without the intention of accepting the Sacrament). But can private writings which remain purely private (not witnessed by some public official) prove *for* the petitioner? Logically, the answer must be in the negative; the legislator in granting the privilege of the shortened process of canon 1990 specified the conditions for the use of the privilege and these should be followed; accordingly, as the impediments of canon 1990 are such as may all be proved by authentic (public) documents it seems logical to maintain that the Legislator wished to restrict the shortened process to those instances when such authentic or authenticated documents were available.

Nevertheless there are authors who would admit purely private writings as proof in canon 1990, either making explicit mention of them [39] or indirectly by considering *authentico* as meaning genuine, though not necessarily of a public character.[40] Although they do not advance reasons for their views, there is at least extrinsic probability to their opinion and so purely private writings may be cautiously admitted under canon 1990.

Certo. It is to be expected that the document should contain sound proof, if it is to be used in a process which has been shorn of most of the safeguards for obtaining the truth. Generally, the word *certo* is taken in this sense, viz., the document must clearly refer to the impediment alleged as the cause of the nullity and to the person or persons involved in this invalid marriage. For this latter point, it is evident that the document can not speak up to identify the petitioner or defendant and accordingly, some proof must be brought to identify the person, e. g., the testimony of two reliable witnesses that this petitioner or defendant is the same as the one named in the document.

---

39 Payen, *De Matrimonio,* III, n. 2722, 1, b; Triebs "Actio ex cc. 1990-92 Iudicialis Probatur", *Periodica,* XX (1931), 100*-101*.

40 Blat, *De Processibus,* IV, n. 551; Lydon, *Marriage Legislation,* p. 363.

Quod nulli contradictioni vel exceptioni obnoxium est. These words define the meaning of *certo,* viz., the document will be satisfactory if there is nothing in it which may be contradicted or to which exception may be taken. What this means must be determined in each case: whether exception should be taken against the document depends on circumstances surrounding it and on its own appearance and can hardly be defined in theory. Merely a possibility of falsification or error is not grounds for contradicting or taking exception; there should be positive grounds for suspecting the genuine character or the truth contained,[41] e. g., the church seal is missing or the party appears older than the dates marked on the documents or the letters were composed at a time that may be suspected. At times, it may be necessary to test the documents as outlined in canon 1800, with the help of a handwriting expert; in as much as solemnities are to be omitted under canon 1990, the requirements of canon 1801 will not have to be followed.

2. *The Lack of a Dispensation*

Only a few general remarks are in place here, as more details will be given in the particular application to each impediment, in a following section.

Since it is rarely that the non-issuance of a dispensation may be established by a document (practically this would only be when it was noted that a dispensation had been denied), it is demanded by the very nature of the case that other modes of proof be admitted, e. g., presumptions and testimony. Yet because the parallel between the proofs of the impediment's existence and those of a lack of dispensation seemed to strict (*pari certitudine*) and because the pre-Code permit of using other proofs had been omitted in canon 1990, there was some slight basis for the doubt proposed to the Holy See and answered June 16, 1931, viz., were other proofs than documents admissible to

[41] Cappello, *De Matrimonio,* III, n. 891, 3; Vlaming, *Praelectiones, II,* n. 803; Payen, *De Matrimonio,* III, n. 2722, 1, c.

establish the lack of a dispensation?[42] Thereafter it was officially clear that the words, *pari certitudine,* were meant to refer to the degree of certainty, equal to that had for the existence of the impediment (*nulli contradictioni vel exceptioni obnoxium*) and not to the method of obtaining this certitude; any legitimate method of acquiring certitude, e. g., presumptions or testimony or documents, could be used to determine that no dispensation had been obtained. In taking testimony, the safeguard of an oath regarding the truth of the statements should be invoked; as mentioned before, even a deposition made by non-Catholics before a public notary would suffice, although it will be rarely necessary as the lack of a dispensation may safely be presumed in the case of non-Catholics.

Since the required certainty regarding the non-issuance of the dispensation must be subject to no objection nor exception, special care should be taken in establishing that no dispensation was granted at the time of the marriage nor subsequently; as remarked already, it is not every possibility that will serve as an objection or exception, but only when there is some probability or some reason to believe that the parties approached another Chancery other than their own or that of the place of contract. For non-Catholics, it may safely be presumed that they would not have submitted their petition for a dispensation to the Catholic Church; the fact of the conversion of one or the other of the non-Catholics (learned from conversation and discreet questions) surely occasions a prudent suspicion that a dispensation may have been granted (and therefore the Chancery of that diocese wherein the conversion occurred should be approached); a Mission attended by the parties to mixed marriages or Catholic marriages, would give grounds for the probability of a convalidation. Just because the parties lived in a number of dioceses does not seem to be sufficient reason to investigate the

---

[42] "Utrum par certitudo de qua in canone 1990, haberi possit tantum ex certo et authentico documento;—an etiam ex alio legitimo. Resp. Negative ad primam partem;—affiirmative ad secundam" Pontiff. Commiss., 16 Jun. 1931—*AAS*, XXIII (1931), 353.

records of all those Chanceries, unless there should be some positive reason for supposing that one or other of these Chanceries had been approached.

Once a record of a granted dispensation is revealed, it should be presumed that the dispensation was validly granted; e. g., that the alleged cause was just and that the *cautiones* (if a case of disparity of worship) had been tendered and accepted; hence ordinarily the invalidity of the marriage may not be declared when a record of a necessary dispensation is found. At times, however, the basis for the petition of nullity is the very dispensation of which a record is extant, but which is claimed to have been conceded invalidly. Undoubtedly, an impediment invalid for one or another reason is equivalent to no dispensation at all so that the impediments would persist [43] and marriages contracted in the presence of such diriment impediments would remain invalid. Can such a plea of nullity be handled under canon 1990? It would seem that such a petition is admissible, as long as certitude can be obtained.[44] On the other hand the short process of canon 1990 would hardly be adequate to determine, e. g., whether the Catholic party really would have apostatized if the dispensation had been denied or whether there really was a well-grounded hope of the conversion of the non-Catholic party. But where it could be easily established by a document or by simple testimony of qualified witnesses that the dispensation was invalid because of a fictitious cause or because the *cautiones* (in a disparity of cult case) had been neglected or refused, there seems to be no reason to subject the case to the regular matrimonial trial. An example to illustrate the use of documents could be the following: a priest seeks and obtains a dispensation submitting as the cause, *the fear of a civil mar-*

---

[43] Canon 1054; if the reason for the invalid dispensation should be the submission of a fictitious cause, then only impediments of the major grade would persist.

[44] Payen, *De Matrimonio*, III, n. 2722, 3. Before the Code, the summary trial could be used for cases where the *cautiones* had been neglected or refused; S. C. S. Off., June 21, 1912—*Fontes*, n. 1293.

riage; later it is discovered that the parties had previously contracted civilly (unknown to the priest) as is evident from their civil marriage certificates; a simple comparison of the dates will establish that the cause was fictitious and accordingly the invalidity of the marriage may be declared.

Other possibilities of a dispensation arise under the conditions of canons 1043-1045, viz., in danger of death and when an impediment is suddenly detected (*omnia sunt parata*). Regarding the former possibility, in danger of death, there need be no questioning of non-Catholics who, of course, could not have obtained such a dispensation without some attempt at conversion and calling in of a priest; for a mixed marriage or a marriage of two Catholics, a few prudent questions about any serious illness will reveal whether there is grounds for investigating a dispensation given under such circumstances. Once the probability of such a dispensation is realized, an investigation should be made; a record of a dispensation granted *in foro externo* should be found in the matrimonial register of the place of sickness or of the place of the contracting of the marriage (canon 1046); a record of a dispensation *in foro interno non sacramentali* should be found in a special register in the Chancery (*a pari* from canon 1047); in the absence of such records the testimony of the priest who attended the sick person, regarding the possible dispensation, will suffice. Of course, if it is evident that the priest acted only as a confessor, there is a conflict of the *forum internum* and the *forum externum* and no information may be obtained from that priest; it would seem that the parties should be questioned (if possible) regarding the convalidation and if they declare that the priest did nothing to convalidate the marriage, then the invalidity of the contract may be declared; it may be so declared because the decision of the judge is to be made on the evidence available in the *forum externum* and if the parties had testified falsely the whole matter is that of the internal *forum*—a question of sinful actions from which the judge is free because he acts in the *forum externum.*

The probability of a dispensation under the emergency conditions of canon 1045 will only exist when a priest witnessed the marriage; in this case, the testimony of that priest regarding a possible dispensation suffices, although a record should be available in the matrimonial register of the place of marriage or in the special secret archive of the Chancery sent there because of the danger of violation of some secret (canon 1045 § 3). Naturally if the priest invoked this canon and professed to have conceded a dispensation, his action should be presumed valid; there need be no investigation regarding the actual impossibility of going to the Ordinary under which the priest had been situated. If this impossibility were challenged as the basis for an invalid dispensation, the case still could be handled under canon 1990 as long as the proof would be the simple testimony of a qualified witness (e. g., if the priest should be willing to testify against himself: "I could have gone to the Ordinary").

3. *The Definitive* (*taxative*) *List of Impediments*

Naturally it is desired that the expeditious process of canon 1990 be applicable to as many cases as possible to save both time and useless expenses; for these reasons, other impediments than the seven listed in canon 1990 have been considered within the scope of that canon, e. g., the impediments of age, public decency, legal relationship; it is believed that such an extension is contrary to the spirit of canon 1990. From the wording of the canon it appears that only the seven impediments there enumerated are to be handled in this shortened process; for the canon does not merely say "whenever an impediment may be established by using a clear and authentic document, the Ordinary may declare the nullity of the marriage," rather it explicitly mentions just seven impediments and emphasizes this enumeration by adding *hisce in casibus*. Furthermore, canon 1990 contains exceptions to the general law requiring a full formal trial for marriage causes and must therefore be interpreted strictly, as referring only to those impediments mentioned.[45]

[45] Canon 19.

Again, the Legislator in formulating canon 1990 evidently considered carefully just which impediments should be included; for, clandestinity appearing in the pre-Code list of summary cases was omitted and two impediments arising from Holy Orders and the Solemn Vow of Chastity, not included in the pre-Code summary process, were added in the Code; it seems to follow then that all other impediments were intended to be excluded and not merely forgotten as has been suggested.[46] Added to the reasons above is the weight of authorities who merely state in one way or another that the list in canon 1990 is final and exclusive.[47] Although this seems by far the more likely view, it cannot be denied that there is a fairly strong minority opinion which would extend canon 1990 to include other impediments; this opinion proffers a reason of expediency, scil., the lengthy forms and costs of a regular matrimonial trial ought to be avoided as often as possible.[48] This reason does not seem adequate to nullify the three canonical reasons urged above and yet, till an official pronouncement is made, there remains some grounds for admitting other impediments under canon 1990; those generally mentioned are the impediments of age, legal relationship (where it has diriment force) public decency, conjugicide (where this crime has been already tried and a sentence handed down regarding the crime).[49]

With these general remarks, it is now possible to turn to the individual impediments and apply these remarks to each impediment in order.

---

[46] Haring, *Eheprozess*, p. 50.

[47] Gasparri, *De Matrimonio*, (ed. nova.), II n. 1283; Payen, *De Matrimonio*, III, nn. 2720-2721; Lanier, *Guide Pratique*, p. 3; Vermeesch-Creusen, *Epitome*, III, n. 296; Triebs, "Actio ex cc. 1990-1992 Iudicialis probatur," *Periodica*, XX (1931), 101*; Noval, *De Iudiciis*, p. 581; Blat, *De Processibus*, IV, nn. 551-552.

[48] Cappello, *De Matrimonio*, (1933), III, n. 891.

[49] Cappello, *op. cit.*, n. 891; Wernz-Vidal, Jus *Matrimoniale*, pp. 842-843. Payen admits the probability of this view, although considering the more common view as far more probable—*De Matrimonio*, III, n. 2721, 2°; Nau, *Marriage Laws of the Code*, p. 226.

4. *Application of the Previous Principles to the Impediments.*

Disparity of Cult

Summary

1. Marriages contracted *before* the Code.
   - a. Cases to be handled under canon 1990.
     1. Marriage of a Catholic and an infidel.
     2. Marriage of a validly baptized and an infidel.
   - b. Cases *not* to be handled under canon 1990.
     1. Marriage of a doubtfully baptized Catholic or non-Catholic with an infidel.
     2. Marriage of two doubtfully baptized (whether Catholics or not).
     3. Marriage of a doubtfully baptized Catholic or non-Catholic with a certainly baptized Catholic or non-Catholic.
2. Marriages contracted *since* the Code.
   - a. Cases to be handled under canon 1990.
     1. Marriages of a Catholic (so baptized or a convert, even though he defected) with an infidel.
   - b. Cases *not* to be handled under canon 1990.
     1. Where there are doubts regarding the baptism in the Catholic Church or conversion thereto:
     2. If "Baptized" party was a:

        Child of a mixed or disparate marriage (without *cautiones*) and baptized by a non-Catholic.

        Child of two non-Catholics and baptized (outside of danger of death) by a Catholic, either against parents' wishes or without provision of Catholic training.

        Child of convert parents who was not presented for supplying of ceremonies or who did not receive other Sacraments of the Church.

Proofs

Record of the baptism of one party (and proof of identity).
Testimony regarding non-baptism of second party.
No dispensation at the time of the marriage nor subsequently.
No *sanatio in radice.*

Of the impediments listed in canon 1990, the most frequent in Chancery practice probably is disparity of cult; for this reason and because of the many possible problems involved, more attention must be devoted to this impediment than to the others. It should be noted that disparity of cult cases because of various doubts must often be sent to the Holy Office; it is well, then, to determine what types of this impediment may be settled by the Diocesan Curia using the short process of canon 1990; in other words, when and how is the required certainty to be obtained for disparity of cult cases.

Disparity of cult may be considered in a wide and in a restricted sense: before the Code, this impediment existed between *any* baptized person and an infidel, whereas under the present law, the one party must have been baptized in the Catholic Church or be a convert thereto.

Before the Code

Marriages of Catholics with infidels before the Code without proper dispensation, were invalid and remain invalid under the Code, so that such pre-Code marriages come under canon 1990. The proofs will be the same as for post-Code disparity of cult cases and will be reviewed later in this article.

Furthermore, the marriages of validly baptized Protestants with infidels, antedating May 19, 1918, were invalid and have not been convalidated by the restriction of canon 1070 § 1; the Pontifical Commission has emphasized this when it declared that marriages are to be judged by the law obligatory at the time of the contract.[50] Such marriages were and remain invalid because

[50] Vis novi Codicis estne retroactiva in his, quae modificantur circa sponsalia et impedimenta tum impedientia quam dirimentia matrimon-

of the impediment of disparity of cult as then constituted; hence, as true disparity of cult cases, they are to be included under canon 1990. It should not be objected that canon 1990 is only for Catholic petitioners, for it has been seen that non-Catholics may be petitioners under canon 1990. To establish this pre-Code form of the impediment for non-Catholics, the baptism of one party and the non-baptism of the other must be determined; here only the question of the non-Catholic baptism is to be discussed as the proofs for non-baptism are applicable to all forms of the impediment and will be reviewed once for all *at the end of this section.* The Holy See has often insisted that each case of a Protestant baptism be investigated; [51] if the investigation reveals clearly that the person had been baptized in a sect known to use a proper ritual, i. e., the proper matter and form, the validity of the baptism is to be presumed.[52] In these cases ,there is excluded any reasonable doubt, i. e., this presumption regarding the validity of the baptism did not resolve a doubt, but presupposed the validity even as the validity of Catholic baptisms rightly administered is presumed; hence, these cases of Protestant baptism do not fall under the restriction of the Holy See to be seen in the following paragraphs. The investigation regarding the proper ritual must center about the rite at the time of the baptism and not about the rite as administered today, even in the same sect (because of changes). The evidence of the fact of baptism should, strictly speaking, be in the form of documents, e. g., a copy from the baptismal records of that sect; however, as testimony is admissible under canon 1990 [53], the statement of two reliable

---

ium ita est . . . contracta impedimenta modificata a novo Codice, nulla dispensatione indigent? *Resp.* "Codici, etiam quoad sponsalia et impedimenta, non esse vim retroactivam, sponsalia autem et matrimonia regi iure vigenti quando contracta sunt vel contrahentur, salvo tamen, quoad actionem ex sponsalibus, canone 1017 §3."—Pont. Commis., 2-3 Iun. 1918 *Dubia (IV) de Matrim.*, n. 6.—*AAS*, X (1918), 346.

51 Schenk, *Disparity of Cult*, 129, n. 41.

52 Schenk, *op. cit.*, 123, n. 22; 129-130, n. 42.

53 cf. *supra*, pp. 87-89.

witnesses as to the baptism may be accepted. In such a case, then, the marriage may be declared invalid upon proof of the non-baptism of the other party and of no subsequent convalidation nor *sanatio*; these two latter points may safely be presumed not to have occurred in the marriage of a Protestant and an infidel, for on the one hand they would not have approached the Catholic Church for a *sanatio* or dispensation (practically self-evident) nor would they be presumed to know that the Code had removed the impediment to their marriage (even supposing they had realized the existence of the impediment) and that canons 1133-1134 require a renewal of consent.

May canon 1990 be invoked when there is doubt whether this supposed Protestant (or supposed Catholic) actually submitted to a baptismal rite or whether he had been baptized validly in a sect not known to use the proper ritual as a rule (i. e., *dubium facti or dubium iuris*)? If there is question of *two* supposedly baptized parties whose baptisms remain doubtful after due investigation, their marriages may not be handled under canon 1990 because the pre-Code presumptions favored the validity of such a marriage; such cases must be referred to the Holy See. In the late 19th century, the decision of the validity of marriages of the certainly unbaptized with doubtfully baptized seems to have come within the competence of the Ordinary; this would seem to follow from this fact that Instructions were sent by the Holy See to *Bishops* regarding presumptions about doubtful baptism.[54] Subsequent interpretations by the Holy See (before the Code) restricted this order so that when there was doubt about the validity of a baptism, the nullity cause of disparity of cult had to be sent to the Holy Office. In other words, that pre-Code final presumption, *dubius baptismus habendus est uti validus in ordine ad matrimonium,* could not be invoked by the Bishops themselves in declaring a marriage invalid and a *fortiori,* it can not be invoked under canon 1990. That Bishops could not declare marriages invalid because of

[54] Cf. Inst., ad Epis. Nequallien., 24 Ian. 1877—*Fontes,* n. 1050; Inst. ad Epis. Savannah, 1 Aug. 1883—*Fontes* n. 1083.

disparity of cult, when doubt persisted about the validity of the baptism, seems clear from these two rescripts, forerunners of canons 1990-1992: the Bishop of Angoulême was authorized on September 5, 1888, to follow a shortened procedure in certain cases, including disparity of cult, with this restriction (*dummodo non agatur de valore baptismi forsitan collati, quo in casu semper recurrendum erit ad Sanctam Sedem*);[55] again, the language of the general interpretation of June 5, 1889 evidently excludes doubtful baptisms (. . . *disparitatis cultus et evidenter constat unam partem esse baptizatam et alteram non fuisse baptizatam*).[56]

If the two parties to this pre-Code doubtful marriage had continued to cohabit after the Code, then their marriage would have become valid. As Cardinal Gasparri points out, the law of renewal of consent upon learning of the invalidity of the previous contract affects only the baptized, but when one party is certainly unbaptized and the other doubtfully baptized, this ecclesiastical law of renewal of consent will not bind (*lex dubia non obligat*). It follows in his opinion that continued cohabitation, even without knowledge of the nullity, would "heal" the marriages of infidels with doubtfully baptized Protestants, as the impediment has ceased with the Code.[57] So much for the marriages which were celebrated before the Code; the nature of the impediment as in the Code must now be reviewed.

After the Code

As was mentioned at the beginning of the previous section, disparity of cult before the Code existed between an infidel and *any* baptized person, and of course this included an infidel

---

55 *NRT,* XX (1888), 632-634; *NRT,* XXVI (1894), 26-28; cf. *supra* pp. 37-38.

56 S. C. Off., 5 Jun. 1889—*Fontes* n. 1118; cf. *supra,* pp. 40-44.

57 Gasparri, *De Matrimonio,* (ed. nova), II, nn. 1191 and 1193; Payen, *De Matrimonio,* II, *Casus* 380, p. 868. Note that in a *sanatio in radice,* the dispensation may be granted even though both parties know nothing of the *sanatio;* hence the original consent must be naturally sufficient for the convalidation.

marrying a Catholic; it is this latter form alone that invalidates marriages contracted since the Code. One party must be unbaptized in the Catholic Church or converted to the Catholic Church, even though he should have fallen away at some time previous to the marriage. Generally there will be no difficulty in establishing the baptism, for baptismal-records as a rule are well kept and a copy of the record is to be accepted as providing full proof.[58] In the absence of properly kept records, or due to some emergency wherein baptism had not been conferred by a Catholic priest or where the infant had been baptized by a Catholic party without the knowledge of the parents, the *fact* of a baptism or the decision whether the person was baptized in the Catholic Church must be obtained by means of testimony or of presumptions.

To prove the *fact* of a baptism when the baptismal record is missing, witnesses may be interrogated; sufficient proof is the testimony of the priest who performed the ceremony[59] or the testimony of several witnesses of the ceremony (e. g., the sponsors or parents) or the testimony of several persons who knew the party as a good Catholic who had received the other sacraments.[60] The testimony alone of the reputedly baptized party would not be sufficient proof, whether he claimed to have been baptized as an adult or to have received the other Sacraments from his earliest recollection since he is disqualified as an interested party.[61] If witnesses be lacking, it seems legitimate to use presumptions to establish the fact of a baptism. The presumptions which would be necessary since the Code are twofold: it is to be presumed that baptism has been conferred on the child of Catholic parents and on the child of a mixed or disparate marriage entered into with the proper *cautiones*. It does not seem legitimate to presume, without any added external

58 Canons 1813, §1, 4°; 1814, 1816.

59 Canon 1791 §1.

60 Canon 1791 §2.

61 Canons 1757, §3, 3°;1758; the rule of canon 779 may not be invoked as in marriage cases there is a *praejudicium*.

indications, that Catholic baptism has been conferred on the child of two infidels or of two Protestants or of a mixed or disparate marriage without the *cautiones.*[62]

When the *fact* of a baptism is settled, it is necessary to decide whether the person has been baptized in the Catholic Church. This decision is important since a person may be free from the impediment, even though baptized under circumstances that would seem to have made him a Catholic. The answer to this question generally gives no difficulty as the "Catholic" party will have been baptized solemnly by a priest at the parents' request or privately by a priest in some emergency. It is true, nevertheless, that difficulties may occur and their solution depends on an investigation of the intention of the party himself if baptized as an adult, or of the parents (at least of one) or of the guardians or of the minister of the Sacrament; as a discussion of the theory is not warranted here, only a practical summary of the possible cases will be submitted; in these cases, there is no doubt regarding the *fact* of the baptism. The following persons are considered as having been baptized in the Catholic Church unless otherwise noted and so held by the impediment of disparity of cult:[63]

1. Adults who have expressed their intention explicitly (regardless of the faith of the minister) or implicitly by arranging baptism with a Catholic priest;
2. Infants (the following applies also to the habitually insane):
   a) Infants of two Catholic parents (*semper et ubique*) regardless of the faith of the minister;
   b) Infants of a mixed or disparate marriage (with the *cautiones*), until the contrary be proved;
   c) Infants of a mixed or disparate marriage (without the *cautiones*) if baptized by a Catholic in danger of death; if baptized by a non-Catholic, the doubt re-

[62] Schenk, *Disparity of Cult,* 104-112.

[63] Cf. Schenk, *Disparity of Cult,* 104-112; Lydon, *Marriage Legislation,* 143-144; Nau, *Marriage Laws of the Code,* 92-94.

mains regarding baptism *in Ecclesia Catholica* and *may not* be resolved under canon 1990.

d) Infants of two non-Catholics, when they have been baptized in danger of death by a Catholic or when they have been presented by parents or guardians (or at least by one of these) to a Catholic for baptism or when they have been baptized by a Catholic (having previously lost their parents or guardians or when these had lost their right over the child or could not exercise it in any way, as long as in the two latter suppositions, provision was made for the infant's Catholic education).[64] It is doubtful whether infants of two non-Catholics have been baptized in the Catholic Church, if they had been baptized by a Catholic against the prescriptions of canon 750 § 2, 1° and 2° (i. e., parents or guardians unwilling or no provision for Catholic education)[65] and so their plea of disparity of cult *may not* be handled under canon 1990.

Beside baptism in the Catholic Church, conversion to the Catholic Church is a basis for the impediment of disparity of cult. At times, baptism is to be conferred on an *adult absolutely* and of course such a one is clearly a convert to the Catholic Church. Nor is there any difficulty when baptism is repeated *conditionally* as long as the conversion is evident; the conversion is established when to the conditional baptism are joined the abjuration of heresy and conditional absolution or, re-baptism being unnecessary, when there is proof of the abjuration of heresy. *Infants,* once baptized in a Protestant sect, are considered converts to the Catholic Church:

1. When the Catholic ceremonies of Baptism have been supplied at the request of at least one of the convert parents;
2. when, "enjoying the use of reason, they have received any of the sacraments, or have made a formal profession of

---

64 Schenk, *op. cit.,* nn. 162-164.

65 Schenk, *op. cit.,* nn. 162-164.

faith with the motive of entering the Church".[66]

3. It is doubtful whether infants become converts *ipso facto* by the conversion of their parents and so disparity of cult remains a doubtful impediment for them and *may not* be handled under canon 1990.

For marriages contracted since the Code, in which doubts regarding the fact of the baptism of one of the parties or regarding *Catholic* baptism remain unsolved after investigation, and after the use of the above presumptions, canon 1070 § 2 directs that the validity of *marriage* is to be maintained; for marriages contracted since the Code, doubtful baptisms may no longer be considered valid, with a view to presuming the presence of disparity of cult and consequently the invalidity of the marriage. All cases of doubtfully baptized Catholics marrying with infidels or with validly or doubtfully baptized Catholics or validly or doubtfully baptized non-Catholics must be sent to the Holy Office.

Voluntary rejecting of, or defection from the Catholic Church does not free that person from disparity of cult, for no one is to profit by his own wrongdoing.[67] As has been remarked, if an infant was licitly baptized in the Catholic Church, he is bound by the impediment of disparity of cult, even though he grows up to be an infidel or heretic. There is no need to discuss the defection of those baptized *against* the rules of canons 750-751, as their very incorporation in the Catholic Church is doubtful; their case must be sent to the Holy See.

Proof of Non-Baptism

It is proper, here, to review the proofs for the *non-baptism* of the infidel partner to the marriage. Evidently, documents are not to be expected to prove this negative fact; the proof must be sought from testimony. The sworn testimony of the party should be taken (when possible); but this alone will not constitute sufficient proof (canons 1757, § 3, 3° and 1758). "Two

---

[66] Schenk, *Disparity of Cult*, p. 118.

[67] Schenk, *Disparity of Cult*, p. 102; Payen, *De Matrimonio*, I, n. 1098.

corroborative sworn witnesses must be submitted. Some may be able to testify for a certain period, for instance, in infancy, but could not testify as to adult age. Parents, relatives, intimate friends of the family, at least seven years older than the party, can testify for the period of infancy; for the period of adult age it must be established that the witnesses were intimate friends of the person in question during the period for which they testify. It will readily be seen how important it is to establish this intimacy and that the whole period must be covered up to the time at least of the marriage.''[68]

Lastly, for the proof of the nullity of the marriage due to disparity of cult, it must be established that no dispensation nor *sanatio in radice* had been granted. For this proof, the records of the Chancery must be searched and it seems that this search should extend only to those Chanceries *through which there is reason to believe* that the parties may have obtained a dispensation or *sanatio*: the testimony of the priest who performed the ceremony that he obtained no dispensation is sufficient proof, at least to establish the invalidity at the time of contract. If no record is found, this absence is ordinarily sufficient proof for the lack of a dispensation or *sanatio*. When, however, a record is found, then the dispensation must be presumed to have been validly conceded and no declaration of nullity may be granted; if the grounds for the declaration was the submission of a fictitious cause at the time of the dispensation, then upon due proof (e. g., ''fear of a civil marriage'' is shown to be false, as the parties had already been civilly married) the nullity declaration may be granted under canon 1990 as this is equivalent to no dispensation. Likewise, if the grounds for the declaration was that the *cautiones* were not asked or were refused, this could be handled under canon 1990 as equivalent to no dispensation;[69] however, since it is doubful whether the *sincerity* of the promise affects the validity of the dispensation, this plea of nullity may

[68] Nau, *Marriage Laws of the Code*, p. 224.

[69] Payen, *De Matrimonio*, III, n. 2722, 3, 1°.

not be handled under canon 1990 as lacking certain proof.[70] That no dispensation was granted under canons 1043-1045 should be established according to the suggestions given above (pp. 95-96).

Holy Orders

Summary

Valid reception of Orders and assumption of the consequent obligations are to be presumed upon proof of the *fact* of Ordination.

Fact of Ordination established by a transcript from Registers of Ordinations.

No dispensation (Chancery Office; nor under canons 1043-1045).

By the positive law of the Church for Latins, no one who has been validly ordained *in sacris* and has assumed the consequent obligations, may contract a valid marriage; *in sacris* refers to the Subdiaconate, the Diaconate and the Priesthood.[71] An attempted marriage by such a cleric is invalid and may be so declared under canon 1990, as long as certainty of the impediment and lack of a dispensation are established.

Proof of the Existence of the Impediment

The fact of the ordination may be easily established by a transcript from the Register of Ordinations kept in the Curia of the place of Ordination[72] or in the Curia of the candidate's own Bishop[73] or from the annotations that should have been made in the baptismal record of the candidate;[74] absence of an-

---

[70] Park, "Insincere Ante-Nuptial Guarantees," *AER,* XCI (1934), 446-459.

[71] Canon 941.

[72] Canon 1010 §1.

[73] Canon 1010 §2.

[74] Canon 1011.

notations in this latter record should not be admitted as proof of the non-reception of Holy Orders, because of possible negligence in making such annotations. If the man be a religious, the transcript may be obtained from the records of his religious home [75] or from the record of his baptism.[76] The validity and obligations of Holy Orders are to be presumed upon proof of the *fact* of ordination unless there should be reason to doubt the ordination because of a faulty rite of defective matter or reason to think that the obligations were not assumed because of grave fear or lack of sufficient knowledge of the nature of celibacy. The subjective conditions may be corroborated by the sworn testimony of the candidate (where possible) who thus testifies against himself, obligating himself clearly to the observance either of his Order or of the marriage. If the *Defensor* doubts whether the candidate is obliged by celibacy because of lack of sufficient knowledge (rarely admitted in an adult) or of grave fear (canon 214) or of the mode of the conferring of the Order, the case may not be handled under canon 1990; a previous decision regarding the Holy Orders and the consequent obligations must be made in accord with canons 1993-1998 and the Instruction of the Sacred Congregation of Sacraments.[77]

Proof of no Dispensation

In the second place, it must be clear that no dispensation had been granted. If the one in Major Orders had been dispensed by the Holy See (a rare occurrence), a record will be found in the Chancery either of the Bishop who ordained or of the candidate's Bishop; the existence of such a dispensation may therefore easily be determined. It should be noted that the reduction to or return to the lay state of those in Major Orders, does not free them from the obligation of celibacy so that the impedi-

[75] Canon 1010 §2.

[76] Canon 1011.

[77] S. C. de Sacram. *Regulae Servandae,* 5 Nov. 1931—*AAS,* XXIII (1931), 457-492.

ment continues.[78] Also, when a religious *in sacris* has been released from his solemn vows, he is still bound by the obligation to celibacy arising from his Holy Orders.[79] In danger of death[80] or in the circumstances of canon 1045, a dispensation may have been granted from the Subdiaconate or the Diaconate (not, of course, from the Priesthood). The possibility of a dispensation in accord with canon 1045 will need be considered only if a priest witnessed the marriage and in this case the testimony of that priest regarding the dispensation will be sufficient proof. In every case involving a Subdeacon or a Deacon, it is necessary to determine that no dispensation was granted *in mortis periculo* (Canon 1043). Occasional as are marriages invalid due to this impediment, sickness unto death will be rarer so that the possibility of such dispensation will not be very much of a problem. Certitude on this point will be obtained by prudent questions regarding any serious illness, directed to the one in Major Orders or to others who would know, with the purpose of discovering what priest attended the sick man and by a search of the registers in which that priest would have noted the dispensation (cf. *supra,* pp. 95-96).

Solemn Profession

Summary

Valid profession is presumed upon proof of the *fact* of the Profession.

Fact of profession is established from the Registers of Professions.

No dispensation.

Valid solemn profession (i. e., the solemn vow of chastity) invalidates a subsequent marriage attempted by that religious (man or woman) who made the profession;[81] in one instance,

---

[78] Canon 213 §1- §2.

[79] Canon 640 §1, 2°.

[80] Canon 1043.

[81] Canon 1073; Scharnagl, *Das Feierliche Gelübde Als Ehehindernis*, pp. 92-93.

that of the Jesuits, the simple vow of chastity carries with it the same invalidating effect due to a special privilege granted by Gregory XIII.[82] If such a religious (man or woman) should attempt to marry, his or her marriage would be invalid and could be declared so under canons 1990-1992; for this declaration, two points must be established, viz., a valid profession had been made and had continued to obligate at the time of the attempted marriage.

Documentary proof of the *fact* of a solemn profession may be had from the Register of the religious house wherein the solemn profession was made[83] or in the baptismal register of the candidate's place of baptism;[84] because of possible negligence in filing annotations in the baptismal register, no final argument for the lack of a solemn profession may be drawn from the absence of such a record. If the man, in addition, had been ordained *in sacris,* proof of this will give another ground for nullity. When the record of the solemn profession is in order, it is legitimate to presume that the profession was made validly because of the great care generally devoted to the observance of canonical requirements of profession.

If the *Defensor* should have a reasonable doubt concerning the requirements for a valid profession, viz., age, novitiate, temporary vows before perpetual vows, absence of grave fear or deceit, express profession or competent Superior to receive profession,[85] this doubt must be cleared; generally documents will be available to settle all such doubts.

To establish that this valid profession still obligated at the time of the attempted marriage, four possibilities of the vow's cessation must be excluded. The party must not have been dispensed from his or her solemn profession by a papal indult of

---

82 Const. *Ascendente Domino* 22, 25 Maii 1584—*Fontes* n. 153; Cappello, *De Matrimonio,* 3 ed. (1933), p. 505; Payen, *De Matrimonio,* I, p. 883.

83 Canon 576 §2.

84 Canon 576 §2; 470 §2.

85 Canon 572 §1 and §2; Payen, *De Matrimonio,* I, p. 881

secularization;[86] a record of such a rescript may be obtained from the religious house wherein the candidate had made his or her profession. If the secularization had been granted before the Code it should be read closely as it may have been for one marriage only and so a second marriage, if attempted, would be invalid or the obligation of celibacy may not have been lifted; since the Code, outright secularization once for all, is the rule.[87] The decree of secularization does not *per se* free from the obligation of celibacy binding the religious if he should be *in sacris;*[88] however, the rescript may include a dispensation for a Subdeacon or Deacon (very rarely for a priest) from his obligation of celibacy.[89] Individual Constitutions must be investigated for the effect of any other release from religion, short of secularization, e. g., dismissal.[90]

The party must not have been dispensed from his or her solemn vow in danger of death[91] or under the circumstances of canon 1045; the faculties of these canons cover also the obligation of *celibacy* binding a religious Subdeacon or religious Deacon, but may not be used to convalidate an attempted marriage of a religious priest. The procedure and the form of these proofs may be consulted in the previous section on *Lack of a Dispensation* in relation to canons 1043-1045.[92] The party must not have been implicitly dispensed from his or her solemn vows, by legitimately transferring to a Congregation of simple vows only;[93] the rescript obtained for this transfer from the Congregation for Religious[94] should be sought in the original House of solemn profession or in the House of the simple profession or

[86] Canon 640 §1, 2º.

[87] Cappello, *De Matrimonio,* 3 ed. (1933), nn. 453-454; Gasparri, *De Matrimonio,* (ed nova.), I, nn. 629-631.

[88] Canon 640 §1, 2º.

[89] Gasparri, *De Matrimonio,* (ed. nova), I, p. 380.

[90] Canon 669 §1.

[91] Canon 1043-1044.

[92] *Supra,* pp. 95-96.

[93] Canon 636.

[94] Canon 632.

from the religious himself to whom the rescript is at times given. The obligation of celibacy arising from Holy Orders remains, even after such a release from solemn profession.[95]

The Simple Vows of the Jesuit Society

As noted above, the simple vows taken by the Jesuits (whether these be students for the priesthood or aspirant lay brothers) after the two years of novitiate would invalidate any subsequent attempt to marry; the same invalidating effect exists in the final vows, whether these be simple vows again or the solemn vows taken by certain members of the Society. The record of the profession is to be sought from the party's Provincial House or from the record of the party's baptism.[96] Possible cessation of the impediment arises from a decree of secularization, from dispensation *in mortis periculo* or when *omnia sunt parata,* by legitimate transfer to a Congregation of simple vows which do not have an invalidating effect and in addition, by legitimate dismissal from the Society because its Constitutions so direct.[97] Records of such cessation should be sought as indicated above, under the sections on Holy Orders and Solemn Profession; of course, the obligation to celibacy arising from Holy Orders must always be considered separately, both as to acceptance and as to cessation.

---

95 Gasparri, *De Matrimonio,* (ed. nova), I, p. 380.

96 Schäfer, *De Religiosis,* p. 471, n. 4.

97 Canon 669 §1. A special answer to the Pontificial Commission confirmed the power to dismiss even after perpetual vows. Vermeesch-Creuson, *Epitome,* (1933), I, n. 820.

CHAPTER V

THE PROCEDURE OF CANONS 1990-1992 (Cont.)

ARTICLE II. THE IMPEDIMENTS THEMSELVES (Cont.)

4. *Application of the Previous Principles to the Impediments* (Continued)

Ligamen

Summary

Cases which may be handled under canon 1990:

1. When all three parties to the two marriages are alive at the time of the plea of nullity;
2. When the parties to the second marriage were divorced or separated before the death of the partner to the first marriage;
3. When the parties, who have cohabited after the death of the partner to the first marriage, are baptized.

Cases *not* to be handled under canon 1990:

1. When the parties to the second marriage who have cohabited *after* the death of the partner to the first marriage, are unbaptized;
2. When the validity of first marriage remains doubtful;
3. When the death of the first partner remains doubtful.

Proofs

1. Certificates of first and second marriages (or transcripts of health department records).
2. Divorce records.
3. Death certificate (if case requires it).
4. Transcript of dispensation from the impediment of crime (if necessary).

A marriage is contracted invalidly because of the impediment of *ligamen,* when at least one of the parties was still bound by a former *valid* marriage. This impediment affects all persons, whether baptized or not, in as much as both polygamy and polyandry are prohibited by the natural law.[1] Of course, it is evident that there can be no question of an ordinary dispensation from this impediment; it is only from the application of the Privilege of the Faith or of a dispensation *Super rato et non consummato* that the diriment obstacle presented by a still existing valid marriage may be removed. Accordingly, when the Catholic or non-Catholic petitioner asserts that his or her marriage is invalid because the other spouse was already married, two questions must be settled, viz., whether the former marriage was valid and whether there had been a convalidation in the event of the dissolution of the previous marriage by the death of one of the parties or by the Privilege of Faith or by a *Super rato non consummato* dispensation. For the sake of a clear presentation, four possible cases will be discussed.

A. All Three Parties Alive at the Time of the Plea of Nullity

The first of these cases presupposes that both parties to a previous marriage are still alive at the time that the plea of the nullity of the second marriage is entered. Here it is only necessary to establish that the previous marriage is valid and that there has been no substitution of persons. The primary proof for this is the marriage-certificates of the first and second marriages. If the first marriage had been solemnized before a priest, the validity of that contract can safely be presumed without further ado; that priest in the ordinary course of events would have established the parties' freedom to marry. By comparing the names on the two marriage-certificates (or better still, on copies of the health department records), the identity of the twice-married person may be established and thereafter, the declaration of nullity may be rendered.

[1] Gasparri, *De Matrimonio* (ed. nova), I, nn. 553-558.

When the marriage-certificate reveals that the first marriage occurred before a minister or a civil official, the same assurance of the validity of that contract is not immediately offered. As far as could be discovered, no author has treated this question, viz., how to handle those *ligamen* cases under canon 1990 which involve marriages not witnessed by a priest; if recourse is had to the practice of the Curias, no unanimity is found. One Curia will submit an exhaustive questionnaire covering all *possibilities* of the invalidity of the first marriage; another will question the party on certain grounds of nullity which that Curia has decided have a *probability* of occurring in every *ligamen* case; a third Curia will not make an investigation concerning the validity as long as no probable grounds of invalidity are present in this particular case (e. g., similarity of names, deficiency of age). It is herewith submitted that given the fact of a previous marriage, its validity is to be presumed unless positive reasons offset this presumption.

Canon 1014 expresses a presumption already recognized before the Code, viz., "*matrimonium gaudet favore iuris*"; this rule applies not only to sacramental marriages but also to the marriages of the unbaptized and to disparate marriages, once there is the appearance of a marriage.[2] This presumption is so strong that once given the *fact* of a marriage, the validity must be supposed until some evident cause overthrows the validity;[3] just what such a reason would be will be considered a little later. Evidently in a *ligamen* case this presumption is to be applied to the previous marriage and not, as some *Defensores vinculi* would have it, to the second marriage submitted for the declaration of nullity: for, there is the old rule that

[2] Gasparri, *De Matrimonio* (ed. nova), I, pp. 24-26.

[3] "In primis enim videndum est utrum matrimonium, de cuius existentia missionarius dubitat, possessionem pro se ostendere merito possit. Hoc enim si contingat, perperam a missionario iudicaretur standum ei esse pro invaliditate, cum iura possessionis servanda sint, donec de contrario perspicue constet." Respon. S. C. S. Off., 18 dec. 1872 ad Vicarios Apostolicos Oceaniae Centralis—*Fontes* n. 1024.

priority of time induces a priority of right [4] and besides the favor of the Code's presumption could hardly be properly applied to the second marriage which had taken place against the prescription of canon 1069 § 2 (*"Quamvis prius matrimonium sit irritum . . . qualibet ex causa, non ideo licet aliud contrahere, antequam de prioris nullitate . . . legitime et certo constiteret"*). With the presumption of validity favoring the previous marriage, there is a definite starting point; the former marriage must be considered valid once the fact of a marriage has been established. The parties (at least the partner to the previous marriage) are not obliged to prove that validity because the Code lifts the burden of proof from those who have a presumption of the law in their favor; [5] if this be true, then all the *possible* causes of invalidity need not be discussed and eliminated, for this is equivalent to forcing the parties to prove the validity of the marriage. Still is there to be no challenging at all of this presumption of validity?

The correct answer would seem to be in the affirmative, i. e., at times there will be definite reasons for believing that the previous marriage is invalid and naturally the presumption of validity can not be final until such solid reasons for doubt are investigated and rejected. As indicated above, the marriage-record may reveal such a similarity of names as to induce the probability of consanguinity or that record of the previous marriage may bear the note "Number of Marriage—Second" thus giving grounds for believing in a previous *ligamen;* such probabilities of invalidity must be resolved before the declaration of nullity may be rendered. Until there is ground for a solid probability of invalidity, there should be no scruples in applying the presumption of validity sanctioned by the Church; to endeavor to establish (prove) such a presumption by eliminating all *possibilities* of nullity is contrary to the nature of a presumption. As a confirmation of this view, the following remarks may be in order. No one may deny that in every mar-

---

[4] "Qui prior est tempore potior est iure."—Reg. 54, R. J. in VI.°

[5] Canon 1827.

riage (even in those witnessed by a priest) there is the possibility and often enough, the probability, of a fictitious or vitiated consent; until such a fault is proved, the consent is presumed valid or corresponding to the words or signs used in the marriage ceremony.[6] According to those who would investigate every possibility of the invalidity of the previous marriage, this possibly insufficient consent should be investigated in its turn. Just on this score, it seems that the view of investigating all possibilities must be rejected, for the Church Herself has precluded an investigation of this very fundamental element of the marriage-contract, a possibly faulty consent. Canon 1990 supposes that there exist clear and evident cases of nullity due to *ligamen;* yet, if it had to be proved in every case that the consent was not faulty, there could never be any *ligamen* cases handled under canon 1990 because such a proof is always most difficult and lengthy and not at all consonant with the simplicity of canon 1990. If the Church Herself has precluded an investigation of this basic possibility, it would seem to follow that it is Her wish to stand by the presumption of the validity of a marriage until some good reason is advanced to question the presumption.

Lastly it is necessary, as in all cases, to show that the person who was party to the previous marriage is actually the same person who is party to the succeeding invalid marriage; this identification may be established by a comparison of the names, birthdays, place of birth, etc., appearing on the original marriage license or certificate or health certificate with those on the succeeding marriage license or certificate or health certificate. Proof that the partner of the first marriage is still alive may be obtained from the sworn testimony of several witnesses. As has been remarked before, a copy of the civil divorce from both the first and second marriages should be demanded for the civil protection of the ecclesiastical Curia.

Having established (1) that the previous marriage was valid, (2) that both parties to that marriage are still alive and that one

[6] Canon 1086 § 1.

of them attempted this second marriage, the Ordinary (or his delegate) may declare the nullity of the second marriage in accord with the rules of canon 1990. What must be done if the case is doubtful, will be seen below in the fourth place.

B. Divorce of Second Marriage, Before Death of First Partner

A second case of marriage involving *ligamen* resembles the first case in all respects except that one of the parties to the former marriage has died sometime *after* his or her partner had attempted a second marriage; this case may be considered in a two-fold matter. If the parties to the attempted second marriage are divorced before the death of the partner to the first marriage, the case is comparatively simple. The same proofs as in the first case will be used to prove the validity of the former marriage and the identity of the person supposedly a party to both marriages. It remains only to prove that the divorce of the second marriage occurred before the death of the spouse of the first marriage; of course, this will be seen from a comparison of the dates of the death certificate and of the divorce record. In this way the absence of convalidation may be ascertained and a declaration of nullity may be rendered under canon 1990.

C. Continued Cohabitation After Death of First Partner

When the two parties continue to cohabit after the death of the partner to the former marriage, it is necessary to be certain that no convalidation by renewal of consent took place. In view of this, the second marriage of *two unbaptized* may not be declared invalid as long as they continued to cohabit, for this suffices as evidence of consent even though they might have been ignorant of the invalidity of their marriage.[7] In the case

[7] Payen, *De Matrimonio,* II, n. 2555, 3°; *Casus* 380, pp. 868-870. Gasparri, *De Matrimonio* (ed. nova), II, n. 1190; n. 1193, cf. footnote n. 57, p. 102.

of *two baptized Protestants,* it is safe to *presume* that no renewal of consent occurred and so a declaration of nullity may be granted; as baptized they are held to a specified renewal of consent (canons 1133-1134), yet this will hardly have been made either because they were ignorant that this second marriage was invalid believing that a divorce from the former marriage enabled them to re-marry or because they were not aware that canon 1134 requires a new act of the will, with knowledge of the previous nullity. If one or both parties to the second marriage are Catholics, it can not be presumed, but must be proved, that no convalidation occurred; for the knowledge of nullity because of *ligamen* is presumed as well as the desire to convalidate the marriage, when possible; prudent questioning should reveal whether an attempt had been made to revalidate the marriage (a record will be kept in some parish, as the renewal must be made *in forma publica* (canon 1135 § 1) or to obtain a *sanatio.* The absence of a record of a dispensation from the impediment of crime (i. e., formal adultery with an attempt at marriage, canon 1075, 1°) will not induce the presumption that the second marriage was not convalidated, because this impediment is not always incurred due to the requirement of *formal* adultery.

D. Doubtful Cases

If it is doubtful whether the first partner has died or not, sometime after the second marriage was invalidly attempted, the marriage of two *unbaptized* may not be declared invalid, for it would have become valid by continued cohabitation if the first partner had actually died; for the baptized, it is only necessary to decide whether any attempt at convalidation was made —generally no effort will have been made, as long as the death is doubtful, and so the nullity may be declared.

If the doubts raised against the presumption of validity are such as to require lengthy investigation, e. g., the process for *mors presumpta,* or if the doubts regarding the validity or convalidation persist after some investigation, then the second marriage is in turn doubtfully valid. In such cases, the resolution of the case seems beyond the scope of the simple, administrative proceeding of canon 1990 and should be handled by the regular process.[8]

Consanguinity

Summary

Under canon 1990 may be tried marriages:

1. Contracted since the Code and invalid because of consanguinity in all degrees of the *linea recta* and up to the third degree *linea collateralis aequalis.*
2. and pre-Code marriages invalid as above or invalid besides because of relationship of the fourth degree *linea collateralis aequalis.*

Proofs

Baptismal records.
Marriage records.
Health records—birth certificates.
Testimony of two trustworthy witnesses preferably older members of the families.
Chancery Office records of dispensations.

A baptized person is incapable of contracting a valid marriage with any one (baptized or not) related to him by blood in *any* degree of the *linea recta* or within the *third* degree of the *linea collateralis aequalis* inclusive.[9] Before the Code, this diriment impediment extended to the fourth degree of the *linea collateralis aequalis*[10] so that a marriage between a baptized

[8] Indications of a rather new procedure in the treating of difficult, positive doubts should be reviewed in: Manning, *Presumptions of Law in Marriage Cases,* Washington, D. C., 1935, pp. 53-67.

[9] Canon 1076 § 1 and § 2.

[10] Before the Code the longer line determined the degree as now and so there was no impediment in fourth mixed with fifth. Ojetti, *De Personis,* pp. 61-63.

person and such a relative (third cousin) was invalid and may be so declared under canon 1990 given proper proofs of no convalidation and of no *sanatio*. Whether the impediment, before the Code, extended to all degrees of the *linea recta* or only to the fourth degree is merely an academic question, for a marriage between a person and his or her great-great-great-grandparent (i. e., the fifth degree) is for all intents and purposes impossible in these modern days.

Infidels

Canon 1990 generally will not be invoked for the marriages of two infidels: the only certain impediment for the unbaptized is that of the first degree *linea recta* and this most likely will never occur in Chancery practice; for the invalidating force for the unbaptized of the other degrees of the *linea recta* and of the first degree of the *linea collateralis*, there are opinions for and against, so that the certainty of invalidity required under canon 1990 can not be obtained. If, however, it should be clear that the civil law has attached an invalidating character to its prohibitions of certain consanguineous marriages, such attempted unions of two unbaptized are invalid and could be so declared under canon 1990, i. e., when such marriages might come to have some relation to a baptized party (e. g., in an attack on a second marriage of one of the infidel parties with a baptized person or when one of the infidels wished to marry a Catholic, even without being baptized).

The Baptized

The impediment arising in the *linea recta* need hardly be considered, as of infrequent occurrence; is such an unnatural union were attempted, the names on baptismal records or the testimony of two trustworthy witnesses would suffice to establish the relationship of parent-child, grandparent-grandchild, etc.: of course there would be no question of a dispensation nor of a *sanatio*.

For the existence of the impediment, e. g., in the *third* degree of the *linea collateralis aequalis* (for the baptized, whether

Catholic or not), transcripts of baptismal records, of marriage records or of civil health certificates (birth certificates) *back to the grandparents* of the two parties are the best proof. Such records are best, because in them it is customary to identify the party (subject of the record) as the child of —— — —— and —— — —— i. e., the family names of the parents; thus the records of the proper grandparents should coincide in pointing to the common ancestor, the great-grandparent through whom the parties are related in third degree. As such records represent a long span of years, it may be difficult to locate all those necessary; besides, in cases of poorly kept records or deficiencies as to names of parents, certainty may not be obtainable from documents. If a serious effort fails to obtain the records, then and only then may the testimony of two trustworthy witnesses, preferably older members of the family, supply the genealogy or the necessary facts of the relationship. Naturally, for the pre-Code impediment which extended to the fourth degree (*linea collateralis*), the investigation must be carried back another generation; for closer relationship (second degree), the records of the parties' *parents* will point to the common ancestor. As consanguinity passes through illegitimate off-spring,[11] proof would have to be adduced for the relationship of such offspring; unless the names of the child's parents appear in the birth-certificate or baptismal record or unless the relationship had been established by a criminal action in civil courts, the proof of such illicit and secret consanguinity is hardly within the scope of Canon 1990 and should be referred to the regular procedure.[12] Then the possibility of multiple consanguinity may enter, arising in the several ways mentioned in the text-books[13] and may be established by additional transcripts of the type of records mentioned above.

---

[11] Canon 1076 § 1.

[12] Wahl, *Consanguinity and Affinity,* 100-101.

[13] Wahl, *op. cit.,* 21-28.

No Dispensation

There will never be any question of a dispensation from the impediment in any degree of the *linea recta* nor in the first degree of the *linea collateralis.*[14]

For the other degrees of the *linea collateralis,* dispensations are granted and the record of such should be sought in those Chanceries from which there is reason to believe that the parties might have obtained a dispensation either at the time of the marriage or subsequently in view of a convalidation or of a *sanatio* (the possible Chanceries may be learned by discreet questioning); absence of the records is sufficient proof. The validity of the cause will not ordinarily be discussed, for if a dispensation has been granted it is presumed validly granted; however, if the parties make the invalid cause the basis of their plea of nullity it is well to remember that a fictitious cause invalidates a dispensation from the second degree of the *linea collateralis aequalis,* because it is a major impediment (canon 1054) and as this may often be proved by documents, it is equivalent to a lack of dispensation and the marriage may be declared invalid under canon 1990; e. g., the cause *timor matrimonii civilis,* can be shown to have been fictitious by a civil document of a civil marriage already previously attempted.[15] Lastly in the case of multiple consanguinity, a dispensation granted from one *species* of the impediment suffices for the validity of the marriage as long as the unmentioned *species* is of the same degree or of an inferior degree.[16] Before the Code this rule did not apply, so that a separate dispensation would have been required for each *species* of the impediment;[17] if a required multiple dispensation had been overlooked before

[14] Gasparri, *De Matrimonio* (ed. nova), I, p. 345; Canon 1076 § 3.

[15] A fictitious cause does not invalidate a dispensation from the third degree (*aequalis*) or touching the second or first degrees (*inaequalis*), as these impediments are of the *gradus minor* (Canons 1042 § 2, 1°; 96 § 3; 1054). Payen, *De Matrimonio,* I, n. 1451, 3, 10.

[16] Canon 1052.

[17] Payen, *De Matrimonio,* I, pp. 518-520.

the Code, such an invalid marriage could be handled under canon 1990, given the necessary proofs.

There is the possibility of the so-called *virtual* dispensation from the impediment of consanguinity which used to be contained implicitly in the dispensation granted for disparity of cult—a rule surely in use before the Code.[18] Such a virtual dispensation was possible after the Code, at least as late as 1924, when the rule was included in the 1st Synod of China, approved by the Holy See.[19] Gasparri notes that the Holy Office replied *"Certo non constare de praxi"* on March 14, 1928, and so at least thereafter the practice was invalid;[20] that such a virtual dispensation is no longer possible is conclusively established by two subsequent responses of the Holy See.[21]

Two other possibilities of a dispensation are under the conditions of canons 1043-1045. As indicated already, the conditions of canon 1045 will be realized only if a priest witnessed the marriage and in this case, the testimony of that priest regarding the dispensation will be sufficient proof. Certitude that no dispensation *in mortis periculo* may be obtained in the same way as outlined above in the section on *Lack of Dispensation* (pp. 95-96).

Affinity

Summary

Cases of affinity to be handled under canon 1990:

All cases of affinity arising under the Code's legislation.

Pre-Code impediment of licit affinity.

Pre-Code impediment of illicit affinity, arising from an invalid marriage that lacked the due form.

---

[18] S. C. S. Off., Instruct. ad Archiep. Quebecen., 16 Sept. 1824.—*Fontes*, n. 866 (n. 2); Wernz, *Ius Decretalium*, p. 646; Gasparri, *De Matrimonio* (1904), I, n. 700; Payen, *De Matrimonio*, I, pp. 776-779.

[19] Canon 396 Concilii Sinensis, 1924.

[20] Gasparri, *De Matrimonio* (ed. nova), I, n. 594.

[21] Sartori, *Enchiridion Canonicum*, ad can. 1071, pp. 145-147; Bouscaren, *The Canon Law Digest*, pp. 512-513.

Pre-Code impediment of illicit affinity arising from *copula* outside of any sort of a marriage can *not* be handled under canon 1990.

Proofs

Affinity under the Code:

Proof of a valid marriage (marriage records and freedom to marry);

Baptismal records of both parties to first marriage;

Proofs of the forbidden degree of consanguinity between the deceased partner and the partner to the second marriage;

Proof of no dispensation nor convalidation nor *sanatio.*

Affinity before the Code:

Proof of the observance of the required form, for licit affinity (marriage record);

Proof of the *copula perfecta* (presumptions and offspring);

Baptism record of party who attempted the second marriage;

Proofs of the forbidden degree of consanguinity between the deceased or divorced partner and the partner to the second marriage.

Proof of no dispensation nor convalidation nor *sanatio.*

Since the Code

Existence of the Impediment

Since the Code, the impediment of affinity arises for a certainty only from a valid sacramental marriage (Catholic or Protestant) and invalidates an attemped marriage between a spouse and his or her partner's relatives in all degrees of the *linea recta* and to the second degree of the *linea collateralis.* "This source of the impediment could be a marriage of two persons already baptized or a marriage during which the two hitherto unbaptized parties were baptized or a marriage between a baptizd and an unbaptized in which the unbaptized became converted."[22] The marriage of two such baptized need alone be

[22] Wahl, *Consanguinity and Affinity,* 58.

considered as the basis for the impediment, because of the *dubium iuris* still extant, regarding the meaning of the words, *ex matrimonio rato,* of canon 97 § 1; hence the possible impediment of affinity arising from the marriage of two infidels or of an infidel and a baptized party will never be considered under canon 1990.[23] As *copula* is no longer required, the existence of the post-Code impediment is a simple matter, viz., was that marriage, which is the source of the impediment, a valid contract made by two baptized persons (or baptized subsequently)? Three proofs are necessary: the baptismal records of both parties; the marriage records, e. g., a transcript from the parochial or civil register; the establishing of the parties' freedom to marry (freedom presumed if it had been a Catholic marriage; for marriage of Protestants, the same presumption is valid with the exception of probable *ligamen*—cf. section on *ligamen*) and of the observance of the due form according to circumstances (e. g., canon 1098, 1° and canon 1099 § 2).

As the degrees of affinity are judged by the degrees of consanguinity, these latter must be computed; i. e., if the attempted marriage of *A* and *C* is claimed to be invalid because *B* (A's partner in a previous marriage) was a blood relative of *C*, the degree of this consanguinity must be first determined: for this, the proofs should be those outlined above in the sections on consanguinity (pp. 121-124).

Absence of any Dispensation, Convalidation or *Sanatio*

That no dispensation was granted at the time of the attempted marriage nor subsequently, can be decided by consulting the records of those Chanceries from which the parties might have obtained the dispensation (to be learned by prudent questioning regarding travels, moving, etc.); lack of records will make it evident that the attempted marriage was invalid and never had been convalidated, by the ordinary means of a Chancery dis-

---

[23] The privilege of the Faith (Canon 1127) may be applied in view of this doubtful impediment, but this is not within the scope of canon 1990.

pensation. Once a dispensation is shown to have been granted, it is to be presumed valid; however if the plea of nullity is based on a dispensation invalid because of a fictitious cause, the nullity may be established as such an invalid dispensation is equivalent to an omission of a dispensation for all degrees of the *linea recta* and from the first degree or the first degree mixed with the second degree of the *linea collateralis,* since these degrees constitute a major impediment.[24] Other possibilities of convalidation arise under the conditions of canon 1045 (*omnia sunt parata*) and *in mortis periculo* (canons 1043-1044). As mentioned on several occasions already, the testimony of the priest who witnessed the ceremony according to canon 1045 is sufficient proof of the granting of a dispensation.[25] In danger of death, a dispensation from all degrees of the impediment of affinity may have been granted, with the exception of the *linea recta* degrees once the marriage has been consummated; the record of this urgent dispensation should be found in the Matrimonial register;[26] as suggested before, prudent questioning should reveal whether either of the parties to the attempted marriage had been in danger of death.[27] Lastly, there must not have been any *sanatio in radice;* an investigation should be made in those Chanceries through which such a *sanatio* might have been granted.

Before the Code

Existence of the Impediment

Because the basis for affinity before the Code was *copula perfecta,* this pre-Code impediment is a rather difficult one to be handled; here, only a summary of various opinions will be pre-

[24] Canon 1042 § 2, 2°; Gasparri, *De Matrimonio* (ed. nova), I, n. 724. It follows that a fictitious cause does not invalidate a dispensation from the second degree of the *linea collateralis aequalis;* canon 1054.

[25] Canon 1791 § 1.

[26] Canon 1046.

[27] Cf. above for details, pp. 95-96.

sented in relation to practice, i. e., in relation to the examining of the validity of pre-Code marriages. *Licit* affinity arose from a consummated marriage which at least one of the parties was baptized (either a Catholic or a Protestant); the marriage could have been valid or putatively valid or invalid as long as it had the *vera species*, i. e., as long as it had been celebrated according to the form binding on the parties. A sacramental marriage was not necessary; nor, on the other hand, did the impediment of affinity arise as long as the two parties remained unbaptized. This pre-Code impediment of licit affinity prohibited the baptized party or baptized parties from contracting a valid marriage, with his or her spouse's relatives at least to the fourth degree of the *linea recta* and to the fourth degree inclusive of the *linea collateralis*.[28] *Illicit* affinity arose from a two-fold source, i. e., from *copula perfecta* had in an invalid marriage that lacked even the semblance of a true marriage (no *species*) because the proper form had been neglected [29] and from *copula perfecta* had outside of a marriage, whether in fornication or in adultery.[30] Before the Code, it is true, *affinitas ex copula illicita* was excluded from the lists of impediments that could be handled by a summary process; [31] it has been remarked that this restriction still applies, so that this impediment must be submitted to the regular matrimonial process.[32] It seems that a distinction is in order: if the *affinitas illicita* arose from *copula* that was altogether hidden; i. e., outside of any appearance of a marriage, then it should not be ordinarily handled under canon 1990 because of the difficulty of proving the *copula;* at times, however, criminal prosecution in the civil courts may have followed such an irregular *copula* and the sentence of the civil

---

[28] Cf. Wernz, *Ius Decretalium,* I, pp. 659-661; Payen, *De Matrimonio,* I, nn. 1482-1483.

[29] Wernz, *op. cit.,* pp. 666-667.

[30] Payen, *De Matrimonio,* II, *Casus,* 383, pp. 875-877.

[31] Cf. footnote n. 4, p. 38; footnote n. 8, p. 40.

[32] Wahl, *Consanguinity and Affinity,* p. 101; Lanier, *Guide Pratique de la Procédure Matrimoniale,* p. 3, footnote .

court could be introduced as proof.[33] If, on the other hand, the *copula* was illicit because it had occurred during a marriage which lacked the *species*, but which nevertheless had been celebrated in some public manner (e. g., by a civil ceremony), the illicit affinity thereby produced should come under canon 1990 as capable of being proved *in foro externo;* in fact here the *copula* would be presumed even more readily if the parties had rushed off to a civil ceremony, neglecting an ecclesiastical form to which they were bound. Illicit affinity invalidated an attempted marriage to the second degree inclusive of both the *linea recta* and the *linea collateralis aequalis* (if mixed with the third degree there was no impediment).[34] To establish any form of the pre-Code impediment of affinity (licit or illicit, except that arising outside of a marriage), proof must be had of the baptism of that person who was party to both the first and the second marriages; proof of the first marriage ceremony of that party, as the basis for the impediment; if the parties to the attemped second marriage are related within the second degree, there is no need of proving the validity of the former marriage, as the impediment in the second degree arose even from an invalid marriage. It is necessary to establish that *copula perfecta* took place; as this is the very basis of the impediment its existence must be by all means determined. If the parties have cohabited and have offspring, this is sufficient proof; apart from this external evidence, the facts of a marriage and of cohabitation, even for a short while, produce a natural presumption of intercourse and as long as no doubt is raised as to the *fact* of the *copula* it is to be presumed *perfecta.*[35] To determine whether

[33] Canon 1813 § 2. It is to this *species* of *affinitas illicita* that the Rota decision quoted by Wahl, refers; S. R. R. *Nullitas Matrimonii,* 3 aug. 1922 —*Decisiones,* XIV (1922), dec. XXVI, n. 1 ad finem.

[34] Wernz, *Ius Decretalium,* p. 667.

[35] Canon 1015 § 2—"Copula enim censetur facta secundum communiter contingentia;" Wernz, *Ius Decretalium,* IV, p. 664; Payen, *De Matrimonio,* I, n. 1480; S. R. R. *Nullitas Matrim.* 22 feb. 1921—*Decisiones* XIII (1921), dec. I, n. 2. S. R. R. *Nullitas Matrim.* 12 nov. 1921—*Decisiones* XIII

this *copula* produced licit or illicit affinity, an investigation must be made regarding the form of the celebration of the marriage that may have obligated the baptized party, for if the due form had not been observed the *copula* of that "marriage" gave rise only to affinity in the second degree. The form required under the *Tametsi* and the relaxations thereof, the exemption of Protestants under the *Ne Temere* and the extraordinary circumstances freeing even Catholics from the form,[36] must all be considered to determine what was the due form and whether the marriage enjoyed the *species* (though possibly invalid because of some impediment). The investigation so far has been confined to the previous marriage which was the source of the affinity; it is necessarily lastly, to determine the blood relationship of the partner to that previous marriage with this partner to the second marriage, because the degrees of affinity depend on the degrees of consanguinity: for this investigation, the rules outlined in the section on consanguinity may be consulted.[37]

Once the fact of the impediment has been established, it must be proved that it had not been removed before or after the celebration of the marriage. In the first place let it be noted that no dispensation is required for the marriages contracted since the Code by two parties who had been related within the degree of affinity forbidden before the Code, but abolished by the Code; e. g., Peter and Mary may validly contract a marriage *since the Code* without a dispensation, even though they had been related by the pre-Code impediment of illicit affinity or in the third or fourth degrees of the *linea collateralis* arising from licit affinity.[38] If the marriage had been attempted before the Code and was invalid because of licit or illicit affinity, the absence of a dispensation and of a *sanatio* either before or after the

(1921), dec. XXVIII, n. 2. S. R. R. *Nullitas Matrim.* 3 aug. 1922—*Decisiones,* XIV (1922), dec. XXVI, n. 3.

[36] Carberry, *The Judicial Form of Marriage,* 139, footnote n. 1; 145; 151.

[37] Cf. *supra*, pp. 121-124.

[38] Payen, *De Matrimonio,* I, n. 1483 *ad finem.*

Code must be established: for Catholics, this will require the usual search of those Chanceries through which there is reason to believe that these favors may have been granted; for two Protestants, it may be safely presumed that neither a dispensation nor *sanatio* has been sought from the Catholic Church. Let it be noted that for the third and fourth degrees of licit affinity and for all the degrees of illicit affinity, the dispensation is implicitly contained in the abolition of these degrees by the Code. In these cases, only a renewal of consent would have been necessary according to canon 1133 § 1 and 1135 § 1 because these forms of the impediment were public;[39] Protestants being baptized are *per se* held to a renewal of consent, but are not obliged to observe the juridical form of this renewal (canon 1135 § 1), in as much as they are exempt from the obligation of the juridical form (canon 1099 § 2); it is practically certain that Protestants are ignorant of the Code's requirements in canon 1133 and of the curtailment of the impediment of affinity in canon 97 § 1, so that the proper renewal of consent can safely be presumed *not* to have taken place. It seems that the same presumption is valid for Catholics in this matter of the abolition of illicit affinity and of the obligation of renewal of consent before a priest and witnesses (canon 1135 § 1); a few prudent questions will easily establish such ignorance and hence the presumption. Again it must be clear that no dispensation from the first and second degrees (*linea collateralis*) of the pre-Code licit affinity had been granted under the circumstances of canons 1043-1045; no dispensation may be granted from pre-Code licit affinity *in linea recta* degrees under these Canons.

[39] The impediment of illicit affinity arising from *copula* outside of any show of a marriage was occult; but it does not seem true to maintain that the illicit affinity arising from the *copula* of a marriage lacking the proper form, is occult, notwithstanding Payen's statement; *De Matrimonio,* I, compare n. 1481, 2° with n. 1482, 2.

Spiritual Relationship

Summary

All cases of the pre-Code forms of the impediment as well as the two-fold form under the Code, may be handled under canon 1990.

Proofs

Baptismal record (marriage record for the pre-Code *compaternitas* and *commaternitas*).
No substitution of persons.
No dispensation nor *sanatio in radice*.

Since the Code

Spiritual relationship under the Code arises only from a valid baptism and is a bond preventing a valid marriage between the baptized subject and the one who administered the sacrament and between the baptized subject and the sponsors. Only a baptized person may contract this impediment, whether he be the minister or the sponsor; Protestants may be bound by this bond, under the conditions to be outlined below; naturally an infidel who baptizes a person, e. g., in danger of death, does not contract the impediment. As marriage-cases involving this impediment are of rare occurrence it will be reviewed but briefly.

The Minister

The attempted marriage of a minister of *solemn* baptism with the woman whom he had baptized is null and may be declared so under canon 1990 upon proof taken from the baptismal records (not to mention the grounds of Sacred Orders, as such a minister must be either a deacon or priest) and proof of no substitution of persons.

The same is true for the minister who baptized an adult convert from some sect, privately.[40] Likewise, the minister of valid

[40] Canon 759 §2.

Protestant baptisms (private, because they lack the solemnities of Catholic baptism) attempt marriage invalidly with those whom he or she has baptized; naturally it is only from a *valid* Protestant baptism that this bond arises.[41] It is practically beyond all dispute that private baptism administered in cases of necessity (canon 759 § 1) sets up this impediment between the minister (nurse or doctor or any other person) and the baptized person; Vidal holds to the contrary view, viz., that no impediment arises under these circumstances but his opinion seems to lack probability both historically and *a fortiori* from the fact that the sponsors under the same circumstances contract the impediment.[42] Lastly, if baptism is repeated conditionally, the minister thereof contracts the impediment with the subject only if he had officiated at the previous baptism[43] (surely this will hardly ever occur); if different ministers officiate (as is to be expected), it seems probable that neither contract the impediment, not so much because there is a *dubium facti* (which baptism was valid) as because there is a *dubium iuris* (i. e., whether an *a pari* argument from canon 763 § 2 is licit, i. e., whether or not the Church wishes this impediment to arise for the minister even from that baptism which was valid).[44]

---

[41] "In dubio de validitate baptismi . . . etiam cognatio et consequenter impedimentum dubium ideoque nullum;" Gasparri, *De Matrimonio* (ed. nova), I, n. 754.

[42] "Ceterum . . . practice non agitur nisi de baptismo *privato*, qui forte a matre vel patre, levatrice, medico similibusque personis *in necessitate* fuit collatus, quorum opera in necessitate pro aeterna salute praestita difficulter concipitur in iure Codicis inferre sequelam inhabilitandi ad matrimonium;" Wernz-Vidal, *Ius Matrimoniale*, V, p. 472 (46). Historically: Wernz, *Ius Decretalium*, pp. 744-746; Gasparri, *De Matrimonio* (1904), I, n. 836; Payen, *De Matrimonio*, I, n. 1568, 1°: *a fortiori*, Gasparri, *De Matrimonio* (ed. nova), I, n. 755.

[43] Gasparri, *De Matrimonio* (ed. nova), I, n. 754; Wernz-Vidal, *Ius Matrimoniale*, V, n. 395.

[44] Payen, *De Matrimonio*, I, n. 1567; Cappello, *De Matrimonio*, III, n. 558; Wernz-Vidal, *Ius Matrimoniale*, V, n. 395.

The Sponsors

Catholic sponsors may not marry their god-children validly, without a dispensation from the impediment of spiritual relationship; the impediment no longer arises between the sponsor and the minister of the Sacrament. Even though the rules of the Code regarding the *licit* acting as sponsor should be disobeyed, the impediment is contracted by each and every one who acted as a valid sponsor. Three general questions regard the *valid* acting as sponsor, viz., was the sponsor (or sponsors) competent under canon 765; did he or she intend to act as sponsor and did he or she properly touch the child as directed in canon 765, 5°? If the baptismal record reveals that *this* person (prove the identity of parties) is named as sponsor of a *solemn* baptism, he must be presumed to have acted validly. The same should be said of those who act as sponsors in *private* administration of the Sacrament.[45] From canon 763 § 2, it is evident that no impediment arises when one acts as sponsor in a conditional baptism, unless he or she had been sponsor in the previous doubtful baptism (practically, this will never be the case.) It appears that a non-Catholic (baptized) acting as sponsor in a valid non-Catholic baptism also contracts this impediment, because the basis of the spiritual relationship, valid baptism, is the same for Catholic or Protestant; the restriction of canon 765, 2° ("*Ad nullam pertineat haereticam aut schismaticam sectam*) does not apply to this case, as it is but one of several regulations regarding Catholic baptism.[46]

Of course, it should be established that no dispensation had been granted either through a Chancery or under the conditions of canons 1043-1045 nor a *sanatio in radice.*

---

[45] Canon 762 § 2; Gasparri, *De Matrimonio* (ed. nova), I, n. 755; Payen, *De Matrimonio,* I, n. 1568.

[46] Nau, *Marriage Laws of the Code,* n. 94, 2, c.

Before the Code

Spiritual relationship with the consequent diriment impediment arose, before the Code, from the valid sacraments of baptism and confirmation and prevented a valid marriage:

I. between the baptized or confirmed subject	and	1. the minister 2. the sponsors	3. the spouses of these once the marriage had been consummated.[47]

II. between the parents of the baptized and of the confirmed subject.	and	1. the minister 2. the sponsors

The conditions for contracting the impediment were practically the same as under the Code:

1. Valid baptism must have been administered (solemn or private baptism producing the impediment for the minister, whilst it remained barely probable that private baptism did not produce the impediment for the sponsors);
2. The minister must have been baptized validly (even though he or she was a non-Catholic);
3. The sponsor must have been baptized validly (even though a non-Catholic—i. e., the prohibition of canon 756, 2° did not then exist);
4. The sponsor must have been otherwise competent (i. e., with the use of reason, intention to act as sponsor, appointment by pastor or parents and must have touched the baptized).
5. For the impediment from confirmation, the sponsors must have been confirmed and had to touch the confirmed subject (*in praxi,* no impediment arose if the sponsors had not been duly appointed).[48]

---

[47] Gasparri, *De Matrimonio* (ed. nova), I, n. 752.

[48] Wernz, *Ius Decretalium,* nn. 489-492.

Let it be noted that the impediment could be multiplied before the Code and had to be mentioned in the *preces* for a dispensation [49] and that these multiplied forms of the impediment have ceased as impediments with the Code.

All of the pre-Code *species* of spiritual relationship have ceased as impediments with the promulgation of the Code, with the exception of those *species* found in the Code; so, of those marriages contracted since the Code by those related by the pre-Code forms of the impediment, only those are invalid which are attempted between a baptized person and his sponsor and between a baptized person and the minister of the sacrament.[50] Once the relationship, as existing before the Code, has been proved from baptism or confirmation records (the parents' names generally will appear also on these records), marriages contracted before the Code by those so related are to be held null; for the forms of *compaternitas* and *commaternitas* the marriage certificates of the parents of the baptized may be required to corroborate the parents' names as found on the baptismal record. Before a declaration of nullity may be made, the absence of a dispensation or *sanatio* must be established: for Protestant marriages, this neglect of dispensation or *sanatio* may be safely presumed as well as the failure to renew consent after the Code (i. e., when the species of the impediment had been one of those abrogated by the Code): for Catholic marriages, the usual search for a dispensation or *sanatio* should be made in those Chanceries from which there is some reason to believe that the favor was sought or in the parish of the marriage and the conditions of canons 1043-1045 should be disposed of; failure to renew consent since the Code may be safely presumed (i. e., in those cases wherein the particular form of the impediment had ceased with the Code).

---

[49] Wernz, *op. cit.*, n. 495; Gasparri, *De Martimonio* (1904), I, n. 850.

[50] Resp. Pontif. Commis. 2-3 Junii 1918; *AAS*, X (1918), 346.

ARTICLE III. THE DECLARATION OF NULLITY

Having decided from the proofs submitted that the nullity of the marriage is evident and having heard the opinion of his *Defensor,* the Ordinary pronounces the freedom of the parties. The strict form of the sentence as outlined in canons 1873-1874 and obligatory in certain points under penalty of nullity [51] does not seem to be binding for this pronouncement given under canon 1990; this would be one of the solemnities which the canon directs should be omitted.[52] For the good order of the records, some form ought to be used and of course this can be the form of the regular sentence or as follows:[53]

Formula for a Disparity of Cult Case

Declaratio
Definitiva

N . . . vs. N . . .
Processus Specialis (Canonis 1990) Nullitatis Matrimonii
n . . .

CURIA N . . .

In Nomine Dei. Amen.

1. Revmus N . . ., Ordinarius (vel Delegatus ab Ordinario) in casu nullitatis matrimonii inter N . . . (*domicilium*) et N . . . (*domicilium*), citatis partibus et interveniente N . . . Vinculi Defensore, iuxta normas sacri canonis 1990 sequentem declarationem nullitatis tulit.
2. In Iure: (*Hic adducuntur canones ad casum pertinentes*)
   In Facto: Adsunt documenta certa et authentica:
   (1) De baptismo N . . .

---

[51] Canon 1894.

[52] Cappello, *De Matrimonio,* III, n. 891.

[53] Lemieux, *The Sentence in Ecclesiastical Procedure,* Washington, D. C., 112-113.

(2) De divortio civili obtento.

Adsunt probationes pariter certae:

(3) De non-baptismo N . . . Testes sequentes, de quorum veracitate ex testimonio authentico parochi N . . . (vel N . . . N . . .) constat, auditi sunt: N . . ., N . . ., etc.

(4) De defectu dispensationis super impedimento . . ex testimonio Curiae N . . . et N . . .

(5) De non-convalidatione matrimonii, ex testimonio Curiae N . . . et N . . .

3. Quibus omnibus tum in iure cum in facto perpensis, Nos decernimus et definitive declaramus constare de nullitate matrimonii in casu seu matrimonium in casu invalidum ab initio fuisse. (*Loco, die, mense et anno.*)

✠ N . . . Ordinarius (vel Iudex delegatus ab Ordinario

[SEAL] N . . . Notarius.

The parties are to be made aware of the decision of the Ordinary in any of the methods mentioned in canon 1877, viz., by reading the decision in their presence or by informing them that they may come to the Curia and see the decision for themselves or a copy of the decision may be sent to them. It is well, as is done at times, to add that "this declaration has no civil effects" which will serve as added protection against a civil suit. Undoubtedly the prescription of canon 1988 should also be observed as this may affect the spiritual welfare of the parties; viz., notice of the declaration of nullity should be forwarded to the pastors of the place of the marriage and of the baptism of the party or parties to be added to their marriage and baptismal records.

Besides the liberation from the many formalities of a regular trial, canon 1990 provides a great saving of time due to the dispensation from the mandatory appeal introduced by Pope Benedict XIV; it is only under the conditions of canon 1991 (to be reviewed in the following article) that the *Defensor* must carry the case to a second hearing. Usually there will be no such "appeal" as only evident cases are in practice submitted to the special process of canon 1990; accordingly, once the nullity of the marriage has been declared under canon 1990 and the party or parties have been notified, they are free to remarry immediately if that is their desire. It would seem that the ten-day period customary after the definitive sentence of the regular matrimonial trial[54] need not be observed in these cases of canon 1990, because the nullity is evident and the provision of a ten-day period during which the *Defensor* may "appeal" seems unnecessary; if, as rarely will occur, the *Defensor* wishes to "appeal" he may do it immediately.[55]

ARTICLE IV. THE ACTION OF CANONS 1991-1992[56]

1. *The "Appeal"*

Rarely will there be the necessity of carrying a case, once decided under canon 1990, to another hearing because *in praxi* only those cases are handled under canon 1990 which are of evident nullity. Nevertheless, the Code has provided for an obligatory revision of the decision given under Canon 1990, under certain circumstances; for example, an Ordinary may be satisfied with the documentary proof submitted in a case and may declare the nullity of the marriage against the opinion of the *Defensor;* the *Defensor,* still doubting the existence of the impediment (e. g., whether the baptism had been conferred in the Catholic Church, in a disparity of cult case) or suspecting with some probability that a dispensation had been granted, must arrange that the case be reviewed by another judge.[57] It will not matter which impediment had been the grounds of the invalidity; an "appeal" from a declaration of the nullity of a marriage because of any of the seven impediments of the

[54] Canon 1987.

[55] Cappello, *De Matrimonio,* III, n. 891; Nau, *Marriage Laws of the Code,* p. 226.

[56] The terminology of these canons has been discussed above, in Chap. III.

[57] ". . . provocare tenetur ad iudicem secundae instantiae. . . ." Canon 1991.

canon is to be handled by the local Curia of appeal without the obligation of recurring to the Holy See for disparity of cult cases. Nau remarks [58] that "there is some doubt whether in a case of Disparity of Worship the Metropolitan court is competent" and quotes two authors, Arendt, S.J., and Creusen, S.J., who wrote on this point. However, the former clearly admits that the impediment of Disparity of Cult is to be handled as the other impediments [59] whilst Creusen quoting Arendt makes him say more than he actually wrote: Arendt [60] stated that an appeal must be sent to the Holy Office from the sentence of the Bishop favoring the nullity of a mixed-marriage (not a disparate marriage) because of one or other diriment impediment and Creusen incorrectly extended this statement to include the appeal from a decision under canon 1990 favoring the nullity of a marriage because of disparity of cult.[61]

The canon mentions only the *Defensor* as submitting the case to a review; but if one or other of the parties should be interested in having the case reviewed, it seems permissible for him to petition it; the canon mentions only the *Defensor* to insist that upon him at times falls the *obligation* of submitting the case to a re-hearing.[62]

Evidently the Legislator wished this revision to be made before the judge of that diocese ordinarily the court of appeal for the regular matrimonial trial; this is clear from the uses of these words, *iudicem secundae instantiae.* A similar provision is made for the settlement of an incidental question in the administrative proceeding of suspension *ex informata conscientia.*[63] Hence, the *acta* of the case will be forwarded to the Metropoli-

---

[58] *Marriage Laws of the Code,* p. 227.

[59] Arendt, S.J., "De Exclusiva S. Officii Competentia Circa Matrimonium Mixtum," *Jus Pontificium,* VII (1927), 136.

[60] *Op. cit.,* p. 135.

[61] Creusen, S.J., "De Competentia in Causis Matrimonialibus," *NRT,* LV (1928), pp. 451-452.

[62] Cappello, *De Matrimonio,* III, n. 891, 3; Triebs, "Actio ex cc. 1990-92 Iudicialis Probatur,"—*Periodica,* XX (1931), 102*.

[63] Canon 2189 § 2.

tan Curia or to the Curia selected once for all for appeals by the individual diocese.[64] In as much as it is believed that this process is administrative, the word *iudicem* is to be considered as equivalent to the Ordinary who of course is the judge *par excellance* in his own diocese and not as referring to the *Officialis* by virtue of his office as judge of the regular trial.[65]

When the *acta* are sent on for review (either the original or an authenticated copy), the canon warns that the judge be made aware that this is a Canon 1990 case, for otherwise he might immediately consider the *acta* as invalid on the supposition that the case had been handled in a regular trial and that necessary formalities had been neglected.

Another reason for this warning lies in the nature of the action instituted by the judge of the second instance; if the case has been settled under canon 1990, this judge has merely to review the facts or proofs of the case as presented from the first instance. That his function is merely revisional seems to follow from the wording of canon 1992: the alternative granted is of confirming the results of the first instance or of requiring fuller proof that may be obtained in a regular trial. In other words, is this really a *casus exceptus* due to the evident nullity or must more proofs be sought for which a regular trial is to be instituted? [66]

As mentioned above, this review is a private matter managed by the Ordinary and his *Defensor*; there is no citation of the parties nor are any of the solemnities of the regular trial necessary. It makes no difference how they proceed as long as both the Ordinary and *Defensor* study the case presented by the first judge and determine whether the nullity of the marriage is really evident. If the Ordinary is satisfied with the proofs as clearly establishing the nullity of the marriage, he confirms the

[64] Canons 1594 and 285.

[65] Until the dispute regarding the character of the process is settled, the *Officialis* will also be competent; cf. Response to Curia of Paris, pp. 73-76.

[66] Cappello, *De Matrimonio,* III, n. 891; Payen, *De Matrimonio,* III, n. 2725; Còcchi, *De Processibus,* VII, n. 309, 4.

decision of the first judge and sends his own judgment back to the Curia of the first diocese. In turn, this Ordinary or his Notary should inform the party or parties of their freedom from the marriage; the delay of ten days does not seem necessary in these cases wherein the nullity has been twice declared evident. The proper notifications should be sent to the pastors of the place of marriage and of the place of baptism.[67]

2. *The Remandment of the Case to the Ordinary Procedure*

If the Ordinary agrees with the *Defensor* of the first instance that the case is not clearly proved and that doubts continue regarding either the existence of the impediment or of the lack of a dispensation, he is to send the case back to the first diocese so that it may there be submitted to a regular trial. Although the canon does not consider the possibility, it seems that if the Ordinary of the second instance had confirmed the first sentence against the opinion of his own *Defensor*, this *Defensor* must submit the case to the ordinary marriage trial in the diocese of the first instance and not to any further review after the manner of canons 1990-1992.[68]

It might be objected that the original Ordinary is incompetent to handle the case in a regular trial because he already had seen the case in the first instance.[69] In as much as the Ordinary handled the case originally in an administrative manner, he surely is not incompetent to institute judicial proceedings for the first time, viz., in the regular trial. Furthermore, for those who believe that canon 1990 represents a judicial process, there is no difficulty as the Ordinary is rehearing the case not in *another* grade, but in the same or first grade;[70] besides, canon 1990 contains a special rule so that in any case this constitutes an exception to canon 1571 if it were insisted that the reasoning given above is invalid.

---

[67] Canon 1988.

[68] Connolly, *Appeals,* 190-191.

[69] Canon 1571.

[70] Kay, *Competence,* p. 154; cf. can. 1893, 1987 § 2.

When the *Officialis* had been the judge in first hearing under canon 1990, it seems that the Bishop ought to appoint another priest who will form the tribunal with the two synodal judges. This would be the wiser course, as the *Defensor* might raise a strong exception of prejudice against the *Officialis* acting again on the same case; once a man has weighed the evidence and decided in favor of the nullity of the marriage, it would be difficult to consider new evidence with absolute impartiality.[71]

Generally, it will be to that diocese in which the case was first heard that the Ordinary will remand the case for a regular trial; however, it is just possible that the case had been handled administratively in the first instance without the observance of the judicial rules of competence and under such a circumstance the Ordinary of that first instance may be incompetent to conduct the regular trial and must transmit the *acta* to the competent Curia, in view of the rules of canon 1964.

Another matter to be noted is the following: if a non-Catholic had petitioned the declaration of nullity under canons 1990-1992 (as he is permitted to do),[72] permission must be obtained from the Holy Office before this non-Catholic may be admitted as *actor* in the regular matrimonial trial. This follows from the wording of those rescripts already studied which permit non-Catholics to act in the process of canons 1990-1992: if this process failed to establish the nullity with certainty, the Holy Office prescribes that the matter be submitted to Itself.[73]

---

[71] The Rota recently instructed a Bishop to change the personnel of his tribunal which had decided only an incidental question against the *actor;* the Rota had reversed this decision and remanded the cause itself, the nullity of a marriage, to the Bishop's Court.—Sancta Romana Rota: "II Causae quae eodem anno 1934 transactae fuerunt, vel peremptae, vel quae absque definitiva sententia, ex peculiaribus circumstantiis finem habuerunt; quibus adduntur decreta quoad recursus contra libellorum rejectionem." *AAS,* XXVII (1935), 192.

[72] Cf. *supra,* p. 64.

[73] This is clear from the rescript to the Bishop of Harrisburg which directly dealt only with disparity of cult cases and from the other rescript which included all impediments; in both cases, the wording is: *Si res dubia manserit, Sancto Officio erit deferenda.* Cf. *supra,* pp. 64-66.

In as much as canon 247 § 3 reserves to the Holy Office alone, all cognizance of disparity of cult cases, there is some doubt whether the Ordinary of canon 1992 should remand a doubtful disparity of cult case to the Holy Office or to the Curia of the first instance; Noval directs that the case be sent to the Holy Office because the only exception to canon 247 §3 is the process of canon 1990-1992 and once this process is eliminated, canon 247 is obligatory.[74] However, it is believed that the regular trial even for a disparity of cult case may be instituted by that Ordinary who first handled the case under canon 1990, provided the *actor* is a Catholic. In the first place, canon 1992 makes no distinction among the impediments, so that disparity of cult cases would seem to be included in this rule for remanding a case to a regular trial. Furthermore, canon 1964 regards the Ordinary as competent for all marriage causes save those excepted in the preceding canons; only Pauline prvilege causes are therein reserved to the Holy See so that disparity of cult cases would seem to be within the competence of the Ordinary. Arendt in a special article dealing with an Ordinary's competence in matters connected with mixed marriages, argues that the Bishop as *judex fidei* in his diocese may treat such marriages (e. g., when null because of some impediment) and considers canon 247 § 3 as obliging in this respect, viz., that all *appeals* must be sent to the Holy Office;[75] it seems that the same would be said regarding disparity of cult cases because of the parallel prohibition of these cases in canon 247; as a matter of fact Arendt admits that disparity of cult cases are to be remanded to the Ordinary for the regular trial.[76]

[74] *De Processibus*, p. 584.

[75] Arendt, S.J., "De Exclusiva S. Officii Competentia Circa Matrimonium Mixtum" (can. 247)—*Jus Pontificum*, VII (1927), 131-136.

[76] "Iamvero in istis dispositionibus exceptionalibus non solum nullo mentio fit recursus necessarii ad S. Officium pro appellatione, verum etiam hos videtur potius positive excludi, cum causa simpliciter dicatur deferenda ad iudicem secundae instantiae qui suapte natura et iure expresso est vel metropolitanus, vel S. Rota Romana *imo et iterum ad Ordinarium remittenda.*" (italics mine). Arendt, *op. cit.*, p. 36.

Whether the Ordinary of the original diocese will institute a regular trial or send the case to the Holy See must be determined in each case; some doubts in connection with disparity of cult could be resolved with a lengthier process (e. g., doubts regarding the document of baptism or the fact of the non-baptism of one of the parties); but others are of doctrinal nature (v. g., was this a Catholic baptism?) and should be sent on to the Holy Office for settlement.[77]

If an ordinary matrimonial trial is instituted, all the formalities must be observed and the mandatory appeal must be taken by the *Defensor* from a sentence favoring the nullity of the marriage.

---

[77] Cf. the section dealing with disparity of cult in detail, pp. 101-102; 106.

BIBLIOGRAPHY

Sources

Acta Apostolicae Sedis (AAS), Romae, 1909.

Acta Sanctae Sedis (ASS), Romae, 1865-1908.

Acta et Decreta Concilii Plenarii Baltimorensis Tertii, Murphy, Baltimore, 1886.

Boucaren, T., *The Canon Law Digest,* Milwaukee (Bruce), 1934.

Codex Theodosianus, ed. Kreuger, Mommsen, Meyer, 3 vols., Berolini, 1905.

Codicis Iuris Canonici Fontes, 6 vols., Romae, 1923-1932.

Collectanea Sacrae Congregationis de Propaganda Fide, 2 vols., Romae, 1907.

Corpus Iuris Canonici, 2 vols., Lipsiae, 1922.

Corpus Iuris Civilis, Berolini, 1895.

Mansi, *Sacrorum Conciliorum Nova et Amplissima Collectio,* 51 vols., Paris, 1901-1919.

Migne, *Patrologiae Cursus Completus; series Latina,* 221 vols.; *series Graeca,* 161 vols., Paris, 1859.

Pallottini, S., *Collectio Omnium Conclusionum et Resolutionum . . . Interpretum S.C.C.,* 17 vols. (1664-1860), Romae, 1887.

Quinque Compilationes Antiquae, ed. Friedberg, Lipsiae, 1882.

Regulae Servandae in Processibus super Matrimonio Rato et Non Consummato, etc., Romae, 1923.

Roskovany, P., *Matrimonium in Ecclesia Catholica,* 4 vols., Pestini, 1870.

Sanctae Romanae Rotae Decisiones seu Decisiones, vols. I (1909, printed 1912) to XVI incl. Romae, 1912-1922.

Sartori, P., *Enchiridion Canonicum,* Hankow, ed. 3, 1932.

Thesaurus Resolutionum Sacrae Congregationis Concilii, 167 vols., Romae, 1718-1908.

Reference Works

Ayrinhac-Lydon, *Marriage Legislation in the New Code of Canon Law,* New York, 1932.

(Backofen), Charles Augustine, *A Commentary on the New Code of Canon Law,* ed. 4, 8 vols., St. Louis (Herder) 1921-1929.

Bargilliat, M., *Iuris Canonici Praelectiones,* Paris, 1923.

Benedict XIV, *Omnia Opera,* 17 vols., Aldina, 1847.

Biondo Biondi, *Bullettino dell' istituto di Diritto Romano,* Roma (Instituto di Diritto Romano), 1921.

Blat, Albert, *Commentarium Textus Codicis Iuris Canonici,* 5 vols., Romae, 1921-1927.

Bouix, *De Iudiciis Ecclesiasticis,* Paris, 2 vols., 1883.

Buckland, W. W., *A Text-Book of Roman Law,* Cambridge, 1921.

Cance, M. Adrien, *Le Code de Droit Canonique,* Paris, 1920.

Cappello, Felix, *Tractatus Canonico-Moralis de Sacramentis,* 3 vols., ed. 3, Romae, 1933.

Carberry, John Joseph, *The Juridical Form of Marriage,* Washington, D. C., 1934.

Cerato, Prosdocimus, *Matrimonium a Codice I. C. Integre Desumptum,* ed. 4, Patavini, 1929.

Cerchiari, E., *Sacra Romana Rota,* 4 vols., Romae, 1921.

Chelodi, J., *Ius Matrimoniale,* ed. 3, Tridenti, 1921.

Cicognani, Amleto Giovanni, *Canon Law,* Philadelphia, The Dolphin Press, 1934.

Cocchi, Guidus, *Commentarium in Codicem Iuris Canonici,* 7 vols., Turin, 1925-1930.

Collinet, Paul, *La Procedure par Libelle,* Paris, 1932.

Connolly, Thomas A., *Appeals,* Washington, D. C., 1932.

Corbett, Percy Ellwood, *The Roman Law of Marriage,* Oxford, 1930.

Craisson, D., *Manuale totius Iuris Canonici,* 4 vols., ed. 4, Pictavii, 1895.

Declarevil, J., *Rome, the Law Giver,* New York, 1926.

Devoti, *Ius Canonicum Universum,* 3 vols., Romae, 1837.

Diaz, *Practica Criminalis Canonica,* Venice, 1550.

Durandus, Gulielmus, *Speculum Iuris,* 3 vols., Venice, 1577.

Eichmann, Edward, *Das Prozessrecht des Codex Iuris Canonici,* Paderborn, 1921.

Esmein, A., *Le Mariage en Droit Canonique,* ed., 2, Paris, 1929.

Farrugia, P., *De Matrimonio et Causis Matrimonialibus,* Romae, 1924.

Feije, Henry, *De Impedimentis et Dispensationibus Matrimonialibus,* Louvain, 1885.

Ferraris, L., *Prompta Bibliotheca Canonica,* Parisiis, 1865.

Fourneret, Chaoine P., *Le Mariage Chretien,* ed. 4, Paris (Gabriel Beauchesne) 1925.

Gasparri, Peter, *Tractatus Canonicus de Matrimonio,* ed. 3, Paris, 1904.

———, *Tractatus Canonicus de Matrimonio,* ed. nova, 2 vols., Vaticanae, 1932.

Hostiensis, Henricus, *Summa aurea,* Venis, 1570.

Hurter, *Theologiae Dogmaticae Compendium,* ed. 6, 3 vols., Oeniponte, 1889.

Joyce, George, S.J., *Christian Marriage, London,* 1933.

Jungmann, *Dissertationes in Historiam Ecclesiasticam,* 7 vols., Ratisbon, 1880.

Kay, Thomas H., *Competence in Matrimonial Procedure,* Washington, D. C., 1929.

Knecht, August von, *Handbuch des Katholischen Eherechts,* Freiburg im Breisgau, 1928.

Koeniger-Giese, *Grundzuge des katholischen Kirchenrechts,* Bonn, 1924.

Laboure-Byrnes, *Procedure in the Diocesan Matrimonial Courts of First Instance,* New York (Benziger Bros.), 1928.

Lanier, Henri Ch., *Guide Pratique de la Procedure Matrimoniale,* ed. 2, Paris, 1927.

a Lapide, Cornelius, *Commentarium in Scripturam Sacram,* 26 vols., Paris, 1889.

Leage, R. W., *Roman Private Law,* ed. 3, London (Macmillan & Co.), 1920.

Lega, M., *De Iudiciis Ecclesiasticis* 2 vols., Romae, 1898.

Lemieux, Delisle Antoine, *The Sentence in Ecclesiastical Procedure,* Washington, D. C., 1934.

Linneborn, Joannes, *Grundriss des Eherechts,* Paderborn, 1933.

Manning, John J., *Presumptions of Law in Marriage Cases,* Washington, D. C., 1935.

Maroto, Philippo, *Institutiones Juris Canonici,* ed. 3, Romae, 1921.

Michiels, Gommarus, *Normae Generales Juris Canonici,* 2 vols., Dublin, 1929.

Muniz, T., *Procedimientos Eclesiasticos,* 3 vols., Servilla, 1926.

Mussener, Herm., *Das Katholische Eherecht in der Seelsorgspraxis,* Dusseldorf, 1933.

Noval, O.P., P. Joseph, *Commentarium Codicis Iuris Canonici, Liber IV De Processibus,* Romae, 1920.

Ojetti, B., *Commentarium in Codicem Iuris Canonici,* 4 vol., Rome, 1928.

Payen, G., *De Matrimonio,* 3 vols., Zi-ka-wei, 1928-1929.

Pellegrino, Carolo, *Praxis Vicariorum,* Venice, 1676.

Perrone, John, *De Matrimonio Christiano,* 8 vols., Romae, 1858.

Praelectiones Iuris Canonici, habitâe in Seminario Sancti Sulpitii, Paris, 1859.

Prat, Fernand, *The Theology of St. Paul,* London, 1926.

Reiffenstuel, A., *Ius Canonicum Universum,* 7 vols., Paris, 1864-1870.

Rittershutius, Cunradi, *Expositio Methodica Novellarum Imp. Justiniani,* Florence, 1839.

Roberti, Franciscus, *De Processibus,* 2 vols., Romae, 1926.

Schäfer, T., *De Religiosis ad Normam Codicis Juris Canonici,* Munster, 1927.

Scharnagl, Anton, *Das Feierliche Gelubde als Ehehindernis,* Freiburg, 1908.

Schenk, Francis, *The Matrimonial Impediments of Mixed Religion and Disparity of Cult,* Washington, D. C., 1929.

Schmalzgrueber, *Ius Ecclesiasticum Universum,* 6 vols., Romae, 1843-1845.

Sherman, *Roman Law in the Modern World,* 3 vols., New York, ed. 2, 1924.

Smith, S. B., *Elements of Ecclesiastical Law*, 2 vols., New York, 1882.

———, *The Marriage Process in the United States*, New York, 1893.

Van Hove, A., *De Legibus Ecclesiasticis*, Mechlin, 1930.

Vermeersch-Creusen, *Epitome Iuris Canonici*, ed. 4, 3 vols., Romae, 1931.

Vidal, P., *Institutiones Iuris Civilis Romani*, Prati, 1915.

Vlaming, Th., *Praelectiones Iuris Matrimonii*, ed. 3, 2 vols., Bussum, 1921.

Vromant, G., *Ius Missionariorum, Tom. V De Matrimonio*, Louvain (Museum Lessianum), 1931.

Wahl, Francis X., *The Matrimonial Impediments of Consanguinity and Affinity*, Washington, D .C., 1934.

Wernz, Fr., *Ius Decretalium*, ed. altera, 6 vols., Romae, 1905.

Wernz-Vidal, *Ius Canonicum*, 6 vols., Romae, 1923-1928.

PERIODICALS

American Ecclesiastical Review (AER), Philadelphia, 1889—.

Annuario Pontificio, Vatican City, 1930.

Appollinaris, Romae, 1928—.

Archiv für katholisches Kirchenrecht (AfkK), Mainz, 1857—.

Bullettino dell' instituto di Diritto Romano, Romae, 1891—.

Ephemerides Theologicae Lovaniensis, Lovanii, Brugis, 1924—.

Homiletic and Pastoral Review, The, New York, 1900—.

Il Monitore Ecclesiastico, Romae, 1879—.

Irish Ecclesiastical Record, (IER), Dublin, 1864—.

Jus Pontificium, Romae, 1921—.

Le Canoniste Contemporain, Paris, 1878-1926.

Nouvelle Revue Theologique (NRT), Paris, 1869—.

Periodica de Re Morali, Canonica, Liturgica, Romae, 1905—.

Theologisch-Praktische Quartalschrift, Linz, 1832—.

UNIVERSITAS CATHOLICA AMERICAE

WASHINGTON, D. C.

FACULTAS JURIS CANONICI

No. 93

1935

ALPHABETICAL INDEX

BIOGRAPHICAL NOTE

Edwin J. Kennedy was born in San Francisco, California, January 28, 1908, and attended Jefferson Grammar School in that city. In 1925 he graduated from St. Ignatius High School in the same city and entered St. Joseph's Preparatory Seminary, Mountain View, California. After his course of studies made at St. Patrick's Major Seminary, Menlo Park, California, he was ordained to the priesthood, June 4, 1932. In September, 1932, he entered the Catholic University of America to pursue a graduate course of studies in the School of Canon Law, where he received the degrees of Baccalaureate and Licentiate in Canon Law.

CANON LAW STUDIES

1. Freriks, Rev. Celestine A., C.PP.S., J.C.D., Religious Congregations in Their External Relations, 121 pp., 1916.
2. Galliher, Rev. Daniel M., O.P., J.C.D., Canonical Elections, 117 pp., 1917.
3. Borkowski, Rev. Aurelius L., O.F.M., De Confraternitatibus Ecclesiasticis, 136 pp., 1918.
4. Castillo, Rev. Cayo, J.C.D., Disertacion Historico-canonica sobre la Potestad del Cabildo en Sede Vacante o Impedida del Vicario Capitular 99 pp., 1919 (1918).
5. Kubelbeck, Rev. William J., S.T.B., J.C.D., The Sacred Penitentiaria and Its Relations to Faculties of Ordinaries and Priests, 129 pp., 1918.
6. Petrovits, Rev. Joseph J. C., S.T.D., J.C.D., The New Church Law on Matrimony, X-461 pp., 1919.
7. Hickey, Rev. John J., S.T.B., J.C.D., Irregularities and Simple Impediments in the New Code of Canon Law, 100 pp., 1920.
8. Klekotka, Rev. Peter J., S.T.B., J.C.D., Diocesan Consultors, 179 pp., 1920.
9. Wannenmacher, Rev. Francis, J.C.D., The Evidence in Ecclesiastical Procedure Affecting the Marriage Bond, 1920. (Not Printed.)
10. Golden, Rev. Henry Francis, J.C.D., Parochial Benefices in the New Code, IV-119 pp., 1921. (Printed 1925.)
11. Koudelka, Rev. Charles, J., J.C.D., Pastors, Their Rights and Duties According to the New Code of Canon Law, 211 pp., 1921.
12. Melo, Rev. Antonius, O.F.M., J.C.D., De Exemptione Regularium, X-188 pp., 1921.
13. Schaaf, Rev. Valentine Theodore, O.F.M., S.T.B., J.C.D., The Cloister, X-180 pp., 1921.
14. Burke, Rev. Thomas Joseph, S.T.B., J.C.D., Competence in Ecclesiastical Tribunals, IV-117 pp., 1922.
15. Leech, Rev. George Leo, J.C.D., A Comparative Study of the Constitution "Apostolicae Sedis" and the "Codex Juris Canonici," 179 pp., 1922 .
16. Motry, Rev. Hubert Louis, S.T.D., J.C.D., Diocesan Faculties According to the Code of Canon Law, II-167 pp., 1922.
17. Murphy, Rev. George Lawrence, J.C.D., Delinquencies and Penalties in the Administration and the Reception of the Sacraments, IV-121 pp., 1923.

18. O'Reilly, Rev. John Anthony, S.T.B., J.C.D., Ecclesiastical Sepulture in the New Code of Canon Law, II-129 pp., 1923.

19. Michalicka, Rev. Wenceslas Cyrill, O.S.B., J.C.D., Judicial Procedure in Dismissal of Clerical Exempt Religious, 107 pp., 1923.

20. Dargin, Rev. Edward Vincent, S.T.B., J.C.D., Reserved Cases According to the Code of Canon Law, IV-103 pp., 1924.

21. Godfrey, Rev. John A., S.T.B., J.C.D., The Right of Patronage According to the Code of Canon Law, 153 pp., 1924.

22. Hagedorn, Rev. Francis Edward, J.C.D., General Legislation on Indulgences, II-154 pp., 1924.

23. King, Rev. James Ignatius, J.C.D., The Administration of the Sacraments to Dying Non-Catholics, V-141 pp., 1924.

24. Winslow, Rev. Francis Joseph, A.F.M., J.C.D., Vicars and Prefects Apostolic, IV-149 pp., 1924.

25. Correa, Rev. Jose Servelion, S.T.L., J.C.D., La Potestad Legislativa de la Iglesia Catölica, IV-127 pp., 1925.

26. Dugan, Rev. Henry Francis, M.A., J.C.D., The Judiciary Department of the Diocesan Curia, 87 pp., 1925.

27. Keller, Rev. Charles Frederick, S.T.B., J.C.D., Mass Stipends, 167 pp., 1925.

28. Paschang, Rev. John Linus, J.C.D., The Sacramentals According to the Code of Canon Law, 129 pp., 1925.

29. Pointek, Rev. Cyrillus, O.F.M., S.T.B., J.C.D., De Indulto Exclaustrationis necnon Saecularizationis, XIII-289 pp., 1925.

30. Kearney, Rev. Richard Joseph, S.T.D., J.C.D., Sponsors at Baptism According to the Code of Canon Law, IV-127 pp., 1925.

31. Bartlett, Rev. Chester Joseph, A.M., LL.B., J.C.D., The Tenure of Parochial Property in the United States of America, V-108 pp., 1926.

32. Kilker, Rev. Adrian Jerome, J.C.D., Extreme Unction, V-425 pp., 1926.

33. McCormick, Rev. Robert Emmett, J.C.D., Confessors of Religious, VIII-266 pp., 1926.

34. Miller, Rev. Newton Thomas, J.C.D., Founded Masses According to the Code of Canon Law, VIII-93 pp., 1926.

35. Roelker, Rev. Edward G., S.T.D., J.C.D., Principles of Privilege According to the Code of Canon Law, XI-166 pp., 1926.

36. Bakalarczyk, Rev. Richardus, M.I.C., J.U.D., De Novitiatu, VIII-208 pp., 1927.

37. Pizzuti, Rev. Lawrence, O.F.M., J.U.L., De Parochis Religiosis, 1927. (Not Printed.)

38. Bliley, Rev. Nicholas Martin, O.S.B., J.C.D., Altars According to the Code of Canon Law, XIX-132 pp., 1927.

39. BROWN, BRENDAN FRANCIS, A.L., LL.M., J.U.D., The Canonical Juristic Personality with Special Reference to its Status in the United States of America, V-212 pp., 1927.
40. CAVANAUGH, REV. WILLIAM THOMAS, C.P., J.U.D., The Reservation of the Blessed Sacrament, VIII-101 pp., 1927.
41. DOHENY, REV. WILLIAM J., C.S.C., A.B., J.U.D., Church Property: Modes of Acquisition, X-118 pp., 1927.
42. FELDHAUS, REV. ALOYSIUS H., C.PP.S., J.C.D., Oratories, IX-141 pp., 1927.
43. KELLY, REV. JAMES PATRICK, A.B., J.C.D., The Jurisdiction of the Simple Confessor, X-208 pp., 1927.
44. NEUBERGER, REV. NICHOLAS J., J.C.D., Canon 6 or the Relation of the Codex Juris Canonici to the Preceding Legislation, V-95 pp., 1927.
45. O'KEEFE, REV. GERALD MICHAEL, J.C.D., Matrimonial Dispensations, Powers of Bishops, Priests, and Confessors, VIII-232 pp., 1927.
46. QUIGLEY, REV. JOSEPH, A.M., A.B., J.C.D., Condemned Societies, 139 pp., 1927.
47. ZAPLOTNIK, REV. IOANNES LEO, J.C.D., De Vicariis Foraneis, X-142 pp., 1927.
48. DUSKIE, REV. JOHN ALOYSIUS, A.B., J.C.D., The Canonical Status of the Orientals in the United States, VIII-196 pp., 1928.
49. HYLAND, REV. FRANCIS EDWARD, J.C.D., Excommunication, Its Nature, Historical Development and Effects, VIII-181 pp., 1928 .
50. REINMANN, REV. GERALD JOSEPH, O.M.C., J.C.D., The Third Order Secular of Saint Francis, 201 pp., 1928.
51. SCHENK, REV. FRANCIS J., J.C.D., The Matrimonial Impediments of Mixed Religion and Disparity of Cult, XVI-318 pp., 1929.
52. COADY, REV. JOHN JOSEPH, S.T.D., J.U.D., A.M., The Appointment of Pastors, VIII-150 pp., 1929.
53. KAY, REV THOMAS HENRY, JC.D., Competence in Matrimonial Procedure, VIII-164 pp., 1929.
54. TURNER, REV. SIDNEY JOSEPH, C.P., J.U.D., The Vow of Poverty, XLIX-217 pp., 1929.
55. KEARNEY, REV. RAYMOND A., A.B., S.T.D., J.C.D., The Principles of Delegation, VII-149 pp., 1929.
56. CONRAN, REV. EDWARD JAMES, A.B., J.C.D., The Interdict, V-163 pp., 1930.
57. O'NEIL, REV. WILLIAM H., J.C.D., Papal Rescripts of Favor, VII-218 pp., 1930.
58. BASTNAGEL, REV. CLEMENT VINCENT, J.U.D., The Appointment of Parochial Adjutants and Assistants, XV-257 pp., 1930.
59. FERRY, REV. WILLIAM A., A.B., J.C.D., Stole Fees, X-107 pp., 1930.

60. COSTELLO, REV. JOHN MICHAEL, A.M., J.C.D., Domicile and Quasi-Domicile, VII-201 pp., 1930.

61. KREMER, REV. MICHAEL NICHOLAS, A.B., S.T.B., J.C.D., Church Support in the United States, VI-136 pp., 1930.

62. ANGULO, REV. LUIS, C.M., J.C.D., Legislaciôn de la Iglesia sobre la intenciôn en la applicaciôn de la Santa Misa, VII-104 pp., 1931.

63. FREY, REV. WOLFGANG NORBERT, O.S.B., A.B., J.C.D., The Act of Religious Profession, VIII-174 pp., 1931.

64. ROBERTS, REV. JAMES BRENDAN, A.B., J.C.D., The Banns of Marriage, XIV-140 pp., 1931.

65. RYDER, REV. RAYMOND ALOYSIUS, A.B., J.D.D., Simony, IX-151 pp., 1931.

66. CAMPAGNA, REV. ANGELO, PH.D., J.U.D., Il Vicario Generale del Vescovo, VII-205 pp., 1931.

67. COX, REV. JOSEPH GODFREY, A.B., J.C.D., The Administration of Seminaries, VI-124 pp., 1931.

68. GREGORY, REV. DONALD J., J.U.D., The Pauline Privilege, XV-165 pp., 1931.

69. DONOHUE, REV. JOHN F., J.C.D., The Impediment of Crime, VIII-110 pp., 1931.

70. DOOLEY, REV. EUGENE A., O.M.I., J.C.D., Church Law on Sacred Relics, IX-143 pp., 1931.

71. ORTH, REV. CLEMENT RAYMOND, O.M.C., J.C.D., The Approbation of Religious Institutes, 171 pp., 1931.

72. PERNICONE, REV. JOSEPH M., A.B., J.C.D., The Ecclesiastical Prohibition of Books, XII-267 pp., 1932.

73. CLINTON, REV. CONNELL, A.B., J.C.D., The Pascal Precept, IX- 108 pp., 1932.

74. DONNNELLY, REV. FRANCIS B., A.M., S.T.L., J.C.D., The Diocesan Synod, VIII-125 pp., 1932.

75. TORRENTE, REV. CAMILO, C.F.M., J.C.D., Las Processiones Sagradas, V-145 pp., 1932.

76. MURPHY, REV. EDWIN J., C.PP.S., J.C.D., Suspension Ex Informata Conscientia, XI-122 pp., 1932.

77. MACKENZIE, REV. ERIC F., A.M., S.T.L., J.C.D., The Delict of Heresy in its Commission, Penalization, Absolution, VII-124 pp., 1932.

78. LYONS, REV. AVITUS E., S.T.B., J.C.D., The Collegiate Tribunal of First Instance, XI-147 pp., 1932.

79. CONNOLLY, REV. THOMAS A., J.C.D., Appeals, XI-195 pp., 1932.

80. SANGMEISTER, REV. JOSEPH V., A.B., J.C.D., Force and Fear as Precluding Matrimonial Cnsent, V-211 pp., 1932.

81. JAEGER, REV. LEO A., A.B., J.C.D., The Administration of Vacant and Quasi-Vacant Episcopal Sees in the United States, IX-229 pp., 1932.

82. RIMLINGER, REV. HERBERT T., J.C.D., Error Invalidating Matrimonial Consent, VII-79 pp., 1932.
83. BARRETT, REV. JOHN D. M., S.S., J.C.D., Comparative Study of the Third Plenary Council and the Code, IX-221 pp., 1932.
84. CARBERRY, REV. JOHN J., PH.D., S.T.D., J.C.D., The Juridical Form of Marriage, X-177 pp., 1934.
85. DOLAN, REV. JOHN L., A.B., J.C.D., The Defensor Vinculi, XII-157 pp., 1934.
86. HANNAN, REV. JEROME D., A.M., S.T.D., LL.B., J.C.D., The Canon Law of Wills, IX-517 pp., 1934.
87. LEMIEUX, REV. DELISLE A., A.M., J.C.D., The Sentence in Ecclesiastical Procedure, IX-131 pp., 1934.
88. O'ROURKE, REV. JAMES J., A.B., J.C.D., Parish Registers, VII-109 pp., 1934.
89. TIMLIN, REV. BARTHOLOMEW, O.F.M., A.M., J.C.D., Conditional Matrimonial Consent, X-381 pp., 1924.
90. WAHL, REV. FRANCIS X., A.B., J.C.D., The Matrimonial Impediments of Consanguinity and Affinity, VI-125 pp., 1935.
91. WHITE, REV. ROBERT J., A.B., LL.B., S.T.B., J.C.D., Canonical Ante-Nuptial Promises and the Civil Law, V-152 pp., 1934.
92. HERRERA, REV. ANTHONY PARRA, O.C.D., J.C.L., Legislacion Ecclesiastica sobre el Ayuno y la Abstinencia, 1935.
93. KENNEDY, REV. EDWIN J., J.C.L., The Special Matrimonial Process in Cases of Evident Nullity, 1935.
94. MANNING, REV. JOHN J., A.B., J.C.L., Presumptions of Law in Marriage Cases, 1935.
95. MOEDER, REV. JOHN M., J.C.L., The Proper Bishop for Ordination and Dimissorial Letters, 1935.
96. O'MARA, REV. WILLIAM A., J.C.L., Canonical Causes for Matrimonial Dispensations, 1935.
97. REILLY, REV. PETER, J.C.L., Residence of Pastors, 1935.
98. SMITH, REV. MARINER T., O.P., S.T.LR., J.C.L., The Penal Law for Religious, 1935.
99. WHALEN, REV. DONALD W., A.M., J.C.L., The Value of Testimonial Evidence in Matrimonial Procedure, 1935.

www.ingramcontent.com/pod-product-compliance
Lightning Source LLC
LaVergne TN
LVHW041115090826
844660LV00060B/493

* 9 7 8 0 8 1 3 2 2 2 8 2 0 *